How to Budget and Save when Money is Tight

10 Practical Tips to take Control of your Finances

PUBLISHED BY: Bunyip Publishing

ISBN: 978-1-7638927-0-5

Table of Contents

Introduction

Why Budgeting and Saving Matters When Money is Tight

Money has a way of controlling more than just our bank accounts; it influences our stress levels, our relationships, our opportunities, and even our sense of self-worth. When money is tight, it can feel like you're trapped in a cycle that's impossible to escape. Every paycheck seems to vanish as soon as it arrives, bills stack up faster than you can pay them, and even the slightest financial setback — such as a flat tire or an unexpected medical bill — can throw your entire budget into chaos. It's exhausting, disheartening, and sometimes downright terrifying.

If you're reading this book, chances are you've felt that pressure firsthand. You may be living paycheck to paycheck, struggling to keep up with rising expenses, or feeling overwhelmed by mounting debt. You might have tried to budget before, only to give up when it felt too restrictive or when unexpected expenses blew up your careful plans. It's easy to feel like you're failing — like you're bad with money or just not capable of getting ahead.

But here's the truth: It's not your fault. The financial system isn't set up to make budgeting easy, especially for people who are working hard just to make ends meet. Costs are rising faster than wages, credit cards are marketed as quick fixes, and everywhere you look, you're being encouraged to spend. The system is designed to keep you in debt and dependent. But you don't have to stay stuck.

This book is about helping you take back control of your finances, one small step at a time. Budgeting and saving are not about deprivation or suffering — they're about empowerment. When you know where your money is going and you have a plan in place, you take back the power. You're no longer at the mercy of unexpected expenses and are not stuck feeling guilty or ashamed every time you spend money. You get to decide how your money works for you.

Why Budgeting Feels So Hard (and Why It's Not Your Fault)

Budgeting is one of those things that sounds easy in theory but feels impossible in practice — especially when you don't have much money to work with. The traditional advice around budgeting often assumes that you have plenty of disposable income, a stable job, and a predictable financial situation. But that's not the reality for most people.

If you're barely covering your rent and bills, cutting out coffee and takeout isn't solving the problem. And if you've already trimmed your expenses to the bone, it can feel like there's nothing left to adjust. This is why many people give up on budgeting altogether — it feels like a losing game where the numbers just don't add up.

On top of that, there's a lot of shame and guilt tied to money struggles. If you're in debt or struggling to save, you might feel like you've failed in some way — like you've made bad choices or aren't "good with money." But the reality is that financial challenges are rarely about personal failure. Economic conditions, rising costs, stagnant wages, and lack of access to resources all play a massive role in why money feels tight.

What makes it worse is that financial advice often comes with an undertone of judgment: "Stop buying lattes." "Just stop eating out." "Create a better budget." But none of that advice addresses the underlying problem — that it's hard to make financial progress when you're working with limited resources.

The good news is that you don't need to have a high income or a perfect financial situation to create a budget that works. You just need to shift the approach. Traditional budgeting often focuses on perfection — strict rules, no flexibility, and rigid spending limits. But real life doesn't work that way. An effective budget is one that accounts for real-life challenges, adapts to changing circumstances, and allows room for both needs and wants.

That's what this book is about. It's not about creating a perfect budget — it's about creating a sustainable one. It's not about giving up everything that makes life enjoyable — it's about finding balance.

What This Book Will Teach You

This book is built around a simple but powerful idea: You can take control of your money, even when money is tight. The key is to work with your current situation — not fight against it. You don't need to wait until you have a higher-paying job or until your debt is gone to start budgeting and saving. You can start exactly where you are with the income you have now.

Over the course of the next ten chapters, you'll learn practical, actionable strategies for budgeting and saving — even if you're living paycheck to paycheck. Each chapter will focus on one core principle, guiding you step-by-step through the process of taking control of your finances. Here's what you can expect:

1. **Understanding Your Financial Reality** – You'll learn how to get a clear, honest picture of your financial situation. This includes tracking your spending, identifying financial leaks, and understanding your emotional relationship with money.
2. **Building a Bare-Bones Budget** – We'll create a minimalist budget that focuses on covering essentials first so you can stop feeling like you're drowning in expenses.
3. **Cutting Expenses Without Sacrificing Quality of Life** – You'll discover how to cut back on expenses without feeling deprived. From grocery shopping to entertainment, you'll find creative ways to save money.
4. **Increasing Your Income** – When cutting back isn't enough, we'll explore ways to improve your income through side hustles, freelance work, and negotiating a raise.
5. **Dealing with Debt** – Debt can feel like a weight around your neck. We'll create a realistic plan for paying off debt and preventing new debt from piling up.
6. **Building an Emergency Fund** – Even a small emergency fund can make a huge difference when things go wrong. You'll learn how to save for

emergencies without sacrificing your current budget.

7. **Improving Your Credit Score** – Your credit score matters more than you think. We'll cover how to improve it step-by-step, even if you have bad credit.
8. **Saving for the Future** – Saving isn't just for people with extra money. You'll learn how to save for retirement, invest small amounts, and build long-term financial security.
9. **Mindset and Emotional Control Around Money** – Money stress is real. We'll cover how to manage financial anxiety and develop a healthier relationship with money.
10. **Creating a Sustainable Financial Plan** – The final chapter will help you put it all together and create a long-term financial plan that works with your lifestyle.

What This Book Is NOT

This book is not about quick fixes or miracle solutions. You won't find any advice about getting rich overnight or making huge sacrifices to "prove" you're serious about money. You also won't find any judgment or unrealistic expectations. The goal of this book is to help you create a realistic financial plan that works for *you* — not someone else's idea of the "right" way to handle money.

This book is also not about perfection. There will be setbacks. Life will happen. Unexpected expenses will come up. The goal isn't to create a budget that works perfectly all the time — it's to create a budget that you can adjust and stick to even when things don't go as planned.

Why Now Is the Right Time

There's never a perfect time to start budgeting and saving — but there's also no wrong time. The fact that you picked up this book means you're ready to take control of your money, even if you don't feel ready yet. The hardest part of budgeting and saving is getting started — but once you take that first step, you'll start building momentum.

It's not about having a perfect financial situation — it's about making the most of what you have. No matter how tight things are right now, you *can* create a plan that works. You *can* feel more secure and less stressed about money. You *can* take back control of your financial future.

The first step is simply deciding that you're ready to try. And by picking up this book, you've already done that. Now, let's get started.

Chapter 1

Understanding Your Financial Reality

Section 1.1: Assessing Your Current Financial Situation

Sarah sat at her kitchen table with her laptop open, a cup of coffee growing cold beside her. Her bank statement was pulled up on the screen, and her heart sank as she scrolled through the list of charges. Grocery store purchases, utility payments, takeout orders, and the occasional online shopping spree — it was all there in black and white.

She knew she was living paycheck to paycheck, but she couldn't figure out why. She earned a steady salary, didn't have extravagant tastes, and generally avoided major purchases — so why did it feel like her money was disappearing faster than she could make it?

The problem wasn't that Sarah wasn't making enough money — the problem was that she didn't have a clear understanding of her financial situation. She had never taken the time to sit down and truly assess how much money was coming in and where it was going.

Many people are in the same boat. It's easy to think you're managing your money well because you're keeping up with your bills and not going into overdraft every month — but there's a big difference between surviving and thriving. If you want to take control of your finances, you need to start with the basics: understanding your financial reality.

That means facing the truth about your income, expenses, and spending habits — even if it's uncomfortable. The good news is that once you understand where you stand, you can start making changes that will lead to financial stability and peace of mind.

Listing All Sources of Income

Sarah's first step was to figure out exactly how much money she was bringing in each month.

She had always assumed she knew the answer. After all, her paycheck arrived every two weeks, and she knew roughly how much it was. But when she sat down to add up her total income, she realized she had been overlooking some key sources of cash flow.

Sarah worked a full-time job as a marketing assistant, which brought in $3,000 a month after taxes. That was her primary source of income, so she had always focused on that number when planning her budget. But when she started digging deeper, she realized that she had other sources of income that she hadn't been accounting for.

On weekends, Sarah did freelance writing for a local blog. Some months she made an extra $300, other months it was closer to $500. She also had a small high-yield savings account that generated about $5 in interest every month. It wasn't much, but it was money — and money matters when you're trying to build financial stability.

She also remembered that her grandmother occasionally sent her $100 on her birthday, and her employer sometimes gave her a small bonus at the end of the year. None of these amounts seemed significant on their own, but when Sarah added them all together, they increased her monthly income by hundreds of dollars.

That's the thing about income — most people focus only on their salary, but the small, irregular amounts matter too. Side hustles, bonuses, government benefits, and even cash gifts all count toward your total income. When you start tracking them, you often realize you're making more than you thought.

After adding everything up, Sarah's total monthly income looked like this:

- $3,000 from her salary
- An average of $400 a month from freelance work
- $5 from interest
- An occasional $100 cash gift

Her actual monthly income was closer to **$3,400** — not the $3,000 she had always focused on. That extra $400 was enough to make a serious dent in her savings or debt payments — but because she had never tracked it properly, it was disappearing into her day-to-day spending.

The first step toward financial stability is knowing how much money you actually have. Once Sarah knew her true income, she felt more in control — but the next challenge was figuring out where it was all going.

Tracking All Expenses (Fixed and Variable)

Sarah had always thought of herself as a responsible spender. She wasn't racking up credit card debt or splurging on luxury goods — so why did it feel like her money was evaporating?

The answer became clear when she started tracking her expenses.

Sarah began by listing out her fixed expenses — the regular, predictable costs that hit her bank account every month. Her rent was $1,200, her car payment was $250, and her car insurance was another $100. Then there were the utility bills — $150 for electricity, $50 for water, and $80 for her phone and internet. Her student loan payment was another $150 a month.

Fixed expenses are easy to track because they're predictable. You know they're coming, and the amounts are usually the same every month.

But Sarah's variable expenses were another story.

She started by looking at her grocery bills. She had always estimated that she spent about $300 a month on food — but when she pulled up her bank statements, she realized it was closer to **$500**. The extra $200 wasn't coming from big shopping trips — it was coming from quick runs to the store when she was out of snacks or didn't feel like cooking.

Then there was takeout. Sarah had convinced herself that she only ordered delivery once or twice a month — but the numbers told a different story. Between late-night pizza orders and weekend sushi, she was spending **$250 a month** on takeout alone.

Gas was another issue. She budgeted $100 for gas — but with gas prices fluctuating and extra trips to visit her parents, her actual spending was closer to **$150**.

The biggest surprise, though, came from impulse spending. Sarah had never thought of herself as an impulse shopper, but the bank statements told the truth. A $40 candle from a gift shop, a $60 sweater from a boutique sale, and $15 here and there for coffee and snacks — these little purchases were adding up to nearly **$200 a month**.

By the time Sarah finished adding it all up, her expenses looked like this:

- **Fixed expenses** – $1,980
- **Variable expenses** – $1,100
- **Irregular expenses** – $150

Her total monthly expenses were **$3,230** — which explained why it always felt like there was nothing left over at the end of the month.

Identifying Financial Leaks

Once Sarah had a clear picture of her expenses, the financial leaks were easy to spot.

Takeout was the first problem. Spending $250 a month on food delivery might feel convenient in the moment, but that's **$3,000 a year** — money that could have been going into savings or paying off debt.

Impulse shopping was another leak. Sarah loved the thrill of finding a cute sweater or a new piece of home décor — but those little purchases were adding up to more than **$2,400 a year**.

Subscription services were also draining her account. She was paying for Netflix, Hulu, Spotify, and a couple of fitness apps — but when she sat down and thought about it, she realized she only used Netflix and Spotify consistently. Canceling the others would save her nearly **$40 a month**.

The most surprising leak was from her grocery shopping habits. Running to the store every time she needed something small was driving up her grocery bill. By planning meals in advance and cutting back on convenience items, Sarah realized she could save at least **$100 a month**.

Bringing It All Together

Once Sarah saw her financial reality in black and white, everything clicked into place.

Her total income was **$3,400** — and her total expenses were **$3,230** — which left her with a buffer of **$170** a month. But after identifying her financial leaks, Sarah realized she could easily save an extra **$400–$500** a month by cutting back on takeout, canceling unused subscriptions, and reducing impulse spending.

By taking the time to assess her financial situation, Sarah gained clarity and control. She wasn't "bad with money" — she just hadn't been tracking it properly. Now that she knew where her money was going, she was ready to start making intentional choices — and start building real financial stability.

Section 1.2: Understanding Your Spending Triggers

Sarah sat on her couch, scrolling through her phone. It had been a tough week — work was stressful, she hadn't been sleeping well, and she was feeling overwhelmed. That's when an ad popped up for a flash sale at her favorite clothing store.

Without thinking twice, she clicked the link.

"50% off — today only."

Her heart raced a little as she browsed the site. She found a cute sweater, a pair of jeans, and a jacket she had been eyeing for months. After all, she'd had a rough week — didn't she *deserve* a little treat?

Sarah's finger hovered over the "Buy Now" button for a moment — but she didn't hesitate for long. Within a few seconds, the order was confirmed, and she felt an immediate rush of relief.

But that relief didn't last.

Two days later, when the clothes arrived, Sarah's excitement faded. The sweater didn't fit quite right, and the jeans weren't as flattering as she'd imagined. Worse, when she checked her bank balance, she realized that the $150 she had just spent was money she'd planned to put toward paying down her credit card.

Sarah's story is familiar to almost everyone. Emotional spending — buying things to relieve stress, feel better, or escape from complicated feelings — is one of the most common financial traps.

We live in a world where shopping is easy, fast, and accessible 24/7. With a few taps on your phone, you can have almost anything delivered to your door within hours. Advertisers know this — which is why they design their ads and promotions to tap into your emotions, not your logic.

Emotional spending doesn't just drain your bank account — it creates a cycle of guilt, stress, and more spending. If you want to take control of your finances, you need to understand *why* you spend, not just *how* you spend.

In this section, we'll explore the difference between emotional and practical spending, how to identify patterns in your spending habits, and how to break free from emotional spending once and for all.

Emotional vs. Practical Spending

Sarah had always told herself that she was "bad with money." But the truth was that she wasn't irresponsible — she was an emotional spender.

Emotional spending happens when you buy something not because you need it but because of how you think it will make you *feel.*

Sarah's clothing purchase wasn't practical — it was emotional. She didn't need a new sweater or jacket — she was trying to make herself feel better after a stressful week.

Practical spending, on the other hand, is based on necessity or utility. Practical spending is what happens when you buy groceries, pay your rent, or fill up your gas tank. These are essential expenses that help you meet your day-to-day needs.

The problem is that emotional spending often *feels* necessary in the moment. When you're stressed, sad, or overwhelmed, buying something gives you an immediate sense of relief or satisfaction. Your brain releases dopamine — the "feel-good" chemical — which creates a temporary high. But once that feeling fades, you're left with the same underlying stress — and less money in your bank account.

Sarah's pattern was clear: when she felt overwhelmed, anxious, or bored, her instinct was to shop. She wasn't buying things because she needed them—she was buying them because they gave her a brief sense of control and pleasure.

Understanding the difference between emotional and practical spending is the first step toward changing your behavior. Once Sarah learned to recognize her emotional triggers, she was able to start changing her response.

How to Identify Patterns in Your Spending

After realizing that she was an emotional spender, Sarah decided to track her spending for a month to look for patterns.

At first, it seemed like her spending was all over the place — a coffee here, a pair of shoes there, an impulse purchase on Amazon late at night. But when she dug deeper, patterns started to emerge.

She noticed that she always seemed to overspend right after stressful work meetings. On Fridays, after a hard week, she would order takeout even though she had groceries at home. On weekends, when she was feeling bored or restless, she would browse online stores for sales — not because she needed anything, but because shopping gave her something to do.

Patterns like these are common — and they're often tied to emotions rather than practical needs.

Sarah realized that her emotional spending was triggered by three key emotional states:

1. **Stress** – After a tough day at work, she would justify treating herself as a way to cope.
2. **Boredom** – On lazy weekends, she would scroll through shopping apps just to fill the time.
3. **Loneliness** – On nights when she felt isolated, she would buy things online as a way to feel connected to something.

Emotional spending is often a coping mechanism. The problem is that it only solves the problem temporarily — and it creates a new one by reducing your financial stability.

Once Sarah identified her patterns, the next step was to create strategies to interrupt the cycle.

Steps to Address Emotional Spending

Sarah knew that if she wanted to get her finances under control, she had to change her response to emotional triggers. The key wasn't to eliminate spending completely — it was to learn how to pause, reflect, and choose a different action.

1. Pause Before You Spend

Sarah's first step was to implement the **24-Hour Rule**. Anytime she felt the urge to buy something — especially if it wasn't a necessity — she would wait 24 hours before making the purchase.

This simple rule helped her separate emotional spending from practical spending. When the emotional rush of wanting something wore off, Sarah was often able to see that she didn't actually need the item — and the desire to buy it would fade.

The 24-Hour Rule gives you time to think logically about a purchase instead of reacting emotionally.

2. Find Healthy Alternatives to Shopping

Since Sarah's spending was often triggered by stress and boredom, she created a list of alternative coping mechanisms to replace shopping.

When she felt stressed, instead of shopping online, she would go for a walk or listen to music. When she felt bored, she would reach out to a friend or work on a creative project instead of browsing Amazon.

By giving herself new coping strategies, Sarah started to break the link between emotions and spending.

3. Unsubscribe from Temptation

Sarah realized that many of her impulse purchases were triggered by marketing. When she got a sale notification from her favorite store, it created a sense of urgency — and made her feel like she was "saving money" by spending it.

To remove this temptation, Sarah unsubscribed from store emails and turned off notifications from shopping apps. She also deleted shopping apps from her phone — making it harder to act on impulse.

By cutting off the source of temptation, Sarah made it easier to stick to her financial goals.

4. Create a "Fun Money" Budget

Sarah realized that trying to eliminate all spending was unrealistic. She liked treating herself sometimes — and cutting that out entirely made her feel deprived, which led to more emotional spending.

Instead of forbidding herself from spending, Sarah created a "fun money" category in her budget. She gave herself $100 a month to spend however she wanted — guilt-free.

By creating room for small indulgences, Sarah reduced the temptation to splurge. If she wanted to buy a new sweater, she could — but it came from her fun money budget, not her savings or credit card

Bringing It All Together

After three months of tracking her spending and changing her habits, Sarah's financial situation improved dramatically.

She cut her emotional spending in half by learning to recognize her triggers and replacing shopping with healthier coping strategies. The 24-Hour Rule gave her the space to make better decisions, and her fun money budget allowed her to indulge occasionally without sabotaging her financial progress.

Emotional spending isn't about money — it's about emotion. When you understand *why* you spend, you take away the power that emotional spending has over you. Like Sarah, once you identify your triggers and create new habits, you can take control of your spending — and start building a stronger financial future.

Section 1.3: Setting Realistic Financial Goals

Sarah sat at her kitchen table, a notebook and pen in front of her, ready to figure out her next steps.

She had finally gained a clear picture of her finances. After listing her income and tracking her expenses, she knew exactly how much money was coming in and where it was going. She had also tackled her emotional spending habits and made a plan to cut back on unnecessary purchases.

But now came the hard part: figuring out *what to do next.*

Sarah had always known that saving money was important. She had heard advice about building an emergency fund, investing for retirement, and paying down debt, but it all felt overwhelming. She didn't know where to start or how to prioritize her goals, and deep down, she was afraid of setting herself up for failure.

"What if I create a plan and then I can't stick to it?" she thought. "What if I never reach my goals?"

That's the thing about financial goals — they can feel scary. When you've struggled with money or experienced setbacks, it's easy to feel like you're destined to fail. But the key to success isn't about setting huge, impossible goals — it's about setting *realistic*, achievable goals that build momentum over time.

Sarah didn't need to figure out her entire financial future in one sitting — she just needed to take the first step.

Short-Term vs. Long-Term Goals

Sarah's first mistake had been trying to approach all her financial goals at once.

She wanted to pay off her debt, build an emergency fund, save for a vacation, and start investing for retirement — all while covering her day-to-day expenses. But trying to work on everything at once left her feeling scattered and frustrated.

It was like trying to climb four different mountains at the same time.

That's when Sarah learned about the difference between short-term and long-term goals.

Short-term goals are smaller, more immediate targets — things you can accomplish within the next **three months to a year**. They give you quick wins, boost your confidence, and create momentum.

Long-term goals are bigger, more complex goals that may take **years** to accomplish. These goals require patience and persistence — but they give you direction and purpose.

Sarah realized that she needed to strike a balance between the two.

If she only focused on long-term goals — like building a retirement fund — she wouldn't see enough progress in the short term to stay motivated. But if she only focused on short-term goals — like saving for a vacation — she might not build the foundation she needed for long-term financial security.

To stay motivated, Sarah decided to set one long-term goal and two short-term goals. Her long-term goal was to build an emergency fund with three months' worth of expenses — about **$6,000**. Her short-term goals were to pay off her credit card balance (about **$1,200**) and save for a weekend trip with her friends (about **$300**).

This balance gave her a mix of quick wins and long-term progress — which made the process feel manageable.

Creating Achievable Milestones

The next problem Sarah faced was figuring out *how* to reach her goals.

She knew she wanted to pay off her credit card, save for an emergency fund, and take a vacation — but those numbers felt intimidating when she looked at them as a whole.

$1,200 for credit card debt?
$6,000 for an emergency fund?
$300 for a trip?

It felt like climbing a mountain with no map.

That's when Sarah learned the importance of breaking down her goals into smaller, achievable milestones. Instead of focusing on the full amount, she decided to work in smaller chunks — progress she could measure and celebrate along the way.

For her credit card debt, she set a goal to pay off **$300 a month**. At that rate, she would have the balance cleared within four months. Paying off $300 a month sounded a lot more doable than paying off $1,200 — and each time she knocked out $300, she would feel a sense of accomplishment.

For her emergency fund, Sarah knew that saving $6,000 would take time — so she broke it down into monthly milestones. She set a goal to save **$200 a month**. That meant she would hit her first $1,000 in five months — and seeing that first $1,000 would give her the motivation to keep going.

For her vacation fund, Sarah set aside **$25 a week**. That meant she'd reach her $300 goal in about three months. Knowing that the trip was coming soon — and that she had a clear plan for funding it — made her feel excited rather than stressed.

By creating achievable milestones, Sarah gave herself a clear sense of direction. Every time she hit a milestone, it would reinforce her progress and remind her that she was capable of succeeding.

Adjusting Goals as Needed

Sarah's plan was working — until life happened.

Two months into her debt repayment plan, her car broke down. The repair bill was $600 — and it wiped out half of her emergency fund.

For a moment, Sarah felt like she had failed. She had worked so hard to stick to her plan — and now it felt like all that progress was erased.

But the truth is that setbacks are part of the process. No financial plan is perfect — life happens, and circumstances change.

Instead of giving up, Sarah adjusted her plan.

Since her emergency fund had taken a hit, she decided to scale back her credit card payments temporarily. Instead of paying $300 a month, she lowered it to **$150** until her emergency fund was replenished.

This allowed her to rebuild her emergency fund without completely stalling her debt repayment plan.

She also adjusted her vacation savings. She had originally planned to save $25 a week — but after the car repair, she cut it down to **$15 a week**. It would take a little longer to save for the trip — but that was okay.

Adjusting your goals doesn't mean you've failed — it means you're being smart. Financial plans need to be flexible because life isn't predictable. The key is to adjust your strategy without giving up on the goal altogether.

Staying Motivated

One of the most important things Sarah learned was that motivation comes from progress — not perfection.

After the car repair setback, Sarah considered abandoning her emergency fund goal altogether. But when she checked her savings balance, she realized that she still had **$500** in the account — even after paying for the repair.

That $500 meant she had made real progress — and it gave her the confidence to keep going.

She also started tracking her milestones visually. Sarah created a chart where she could color in sections every time she hit a savings goal or paid down a portion of her debt. Seeing the chart fill up gave her a sense of accomplishment — even when progress was slow.

Most importantly, Sarah reminded herself that this wasn't about perfection — it was about consistency. Some months would be harder than others, but as long as she kept moving forward, she would get there eventually.

Bringing It All Together

After six months of working toward her goals, Sarah had paid off her credit card debt, saved $1,200 toward her emergency fund, and had enough money set aside for her vacation.

The process wasn't always smooth — there were setbacks and adjustments along the way — but Sarah learned that flexibility and persistence matter more than perfection.

Setting realistic financial goals isn't about creating a rigid plan — it's about creating a flexible framework that helps you make consistent progress.

By balancing short-term and long-term goals, breaking them down into achievable milestones, and adjusting when life throws you a curveball, you set yourself up for lasting success.

Sarah's story proves that you don't have to be perfect to reach your goals — you just have to keep going.

Chapter 2

Building a Bare-Bones Budget

Section 2.1: Creating a Minimalist Budget

Sarah had been trying to budget for years — and failing.

She had downloaded countless budgeting apps, followed money-saving advice from social media influencers, and even tried using spreadsheets to track every penny she spent. But nothing seemed to work. Every month, it was the same story: she'd start with the best of intentions, try to stick to her budget for a week or two, and then something would go wrong.

Maybe she'd have a stressful week at work and order too much takeout. Or maybe a friend would invite her to a last-minute weekend trip, and she wouldn't want to say no. Sometimes, she'd just get tired of feeling restricted and give up altogether.

"I'm not good at budgeting," Sarah thought. "Maybe I'm just not the kind of person who can save money."

But Sarah's problem wasn't that she was bad at budgeting — her problem was that she was trying to follow complicated systems that didn't work for her lifestyle.

The truth is that most people overcomplicate budgeting. They try to track every dollar, follow restrictive guidelines, and cut out all "fun" spending — and that's why they fail. A budget that's too rigid or complex is impossible to stick to long-term.

What Sarah needed wasn't a detailed spreadsheet or a complex app — she needed a minimalist budget. A simple, bare-bones plan that focused on covering the essentials, reducing unnecessary spending, and giving her enough flexibility to stay consistent.

A minimalist budget strips away the noise and helps you focus on what really matters. It's not about tracking every detail — it's about creating a simple, repeatable system that helps you spend less and save more.

Separating Needs from Wants

The first step to creating a minimalist budget is figuring out the difference between **needs** and **wants**.

Sarah had always struggled with this concept. When she put together past budgets, she would list things like rent, groceries, and car payments as "needs" — but then she'd add things like Netflix, her gym membership, and takeout meals in the same category.

The problem is that when you treat *everything* like a need, you convince yourself that you can't cut back — and that's how budgets fail.

Sarah needed to get honest with herself.

A *need* is something you can't live without — something essential to your survival or well-being. Rent, groceries, basic utilities, transportation, and minimum debt payments are all needs.

A *want* is everything else — including things that make life easier or more enjoyable. Streaming services, eating out, shopping, hobbies, and entertainment all fall into the "want" category.

Sarah sat down with her bank statements and went through every expense from the last three months.

Her rent? A need. Her internet bill? A need for work. Groceries? A need.

But her $200-a-month DoorDash habit? That was a want — even though it *felt* essential when she was tired after work.

Her Netflix, Spotify, and Apple Music subscriptions? Also wants.

Her gym membership? That one was tricky. It felt like a need because it supported her health — but Sarah realized that she could work out at home for free if she needed to cut back.

Once Sarah separated her needs from her wants, the next step was to build a budget that focused on covering the essentials first.

Allocating Money to Essentials First

Sarah's first budgeting mistake was trying to divide her money between too many categories at once.

She had been setting aside money for savings, debt payments, fun, and groceries — but the problem was that her income wasn't enough to cover *everything* comfortably. By the middle of the month, when money started running low, she would panic — and that's when she would start reaching for her credit card.

The key to a minimalist budget is to cover your essentials first. When you take care of your basic needs, you eliminate financial stress — which makes it easier to avoid emotional spending and impulse purchases.

Sarah's monthly take-home pay was $3,400. Her fixed expenses (the things she had to pay every month) included:

- Rent = $1,200
- Car payment = $250
- Car insurance = $100
- Student loan payment = $150
- Utilities = $150

That added up to **$1,850** in fixed expenses.

Her variable expenses — things like groceries and gas — averaged about **$600** a month. That meant her essential expenses totaled about **$2,450**.

Sarah's first priority was to make sure those essentials were covered every month. She set up automatic payments for all of her fixed expenses and created a separate checking account for groceries and gas — so that money was off-limits for other spending.

By covering her essentials first, Sarah knew that her basic needs would always be met — even if she went overboard in other areas. That gave her a sense of financial security she had never felt before.

After covering her essentials, Sarah had **$950 left over** each month. That money was now divided into three simple categories:

1. **Debt repayment** – $300
2. **Savings** – $400
3. **Fun money** – $250

Instead of trying to micromanage every dollar, Sarah used broad categories. She didn't need to track whether her "fun money" went to coffee, takeout, or a movie — she just needed to stick to the total amount.

If she went over her fun money limit one month, she didn't panic — she simply adjusted the next month.

By simplifying her budget, Sarah gave herself breathing room. She wasn't trying to force herself into a rigid system — she was creating a framework that supported her financial needs while allowing for flexibility.

Finding Budget Templates That Work

Once Sarah had separated her needs from her wants and covered her essentials, the next step was finding a budgeting system that worked for her.

In the past, Sarah had tried using complex spreadsheets and detailed apps — but they made her feel overwhelmed. She would start tracking everything down to the last penny — and then give up after a few weeks.

This time, she wanted to keep it simple.

Sarah found that the **50/30/20 Rule** was a great fit for her minimalist approach.

- **50%** of her income went toward needs (rent, groceries, utilities).
- **30%** went toward wants (fun money and discretionary spending).
- **20%** went toward savings and debt repayment.

For Sarah, this worked out almost perfectly:

- 50% of her $3,400 income = $1,700 for fixed and variable expenses.
- 30% = $1,020 for fun money, dining out, and entertainment.
- 20% = $680 for savings and debt repayment.

Instead of tracking every individual expense, Sarah used broad categories. At the beginning of each month, she moved money into three separate accounts: one for essentials, one for savings, and one for fun money. Once the fun money account ran dry, that was it — no dipping into savings or using credit cards.

For Sarah, this system worked because it was flexible but structured. She didn't have to feel guilty about treating herself — as long as it came from her "wants" category. She also didn't feel deprived because she knew her essentials were covered and her savings were growing.

Bringing It All Together

After three months of following her minimalist budget, Sarah's stress about money had almost disappeared.

She had built up $1,200 in her emergency fund, paid down $600 of her credit card debt, and still had money left over for coffee dates and dinners with friends.

Most importantly, Sarah felt like she was in control for the first time in her life.

A minimalist budget doesn't mean giving up everything you enjoy — it means simplifying your finances so you can focus on what really matters. By covering her essentials first, separating needs from wants, and sticking to broad spending categories, Sarah created a budget she could actually stick to.

Sarah's story proves that budgeting doesn't have to be complicated — it just has to work.

Section 2.2: Tracking Your Spending

Sarah thought she had a pretty good handle on her spending.

After all, she wasn't racking up huge credit card balances, and she always managed to cover her rent and bills. But somehow, at the end of every month, her bank account was nearly empty — and she couldn't figure out where her money was going.

She had a budget in place, but that wasn't enough. She needed to know how well she was sticking to it — and that meant tracking her spending.

Sarah had always resisted the idea of tracking her expenses. It sounded tedious and time-consuming. Plus, she was scared of what she might find. What if it turned out that she was wasting hundreds of dollars a month on things she didn't even need?

But the truth is that you *can't* manage what you don't measure. A budget is like a roadmap — but tracking your spending is how you check if you're staying on course. If you're not tracking, you're essentially driving blind.

Tracking your spending isn't about punishment or restriction — it's about creating awareness. Once you understand your spending patterns, you can adjust them to align with your goals. The process doesn't have to be difficult — in fact, with the right tools and strategies, it can become second nature.

Sarah's breakthrough came when she realized that there are different ways to track spending — and the key was finding the method that worked best for her lifestyle.

Daily, Weekly, and Monthly Tracking Methods

Sarah's first mistake was trying to track her spending in a way that didn't fit her personality.

She had downloaded a budgeting app that required her to log every expense manually — which worked for about three days before she gave up. She also tried to sit down once a month and go through her bank statements — but by that point, it was too late to course-correct.

The key to tracking is to find a rhythm that matches how you naturally think about money.

Sarah realized that there were three basic approaches to tracking: daily, weekly, and monthly. Each method has advantages and challenges — and different people respond better to different strategies.

At first, Sarah tried **daily tracking**. Every evening, she would sit down and write down every dollar she had spent that day. This worked well for creating immediate awareness — but it felt exhausting after a while.

She then switched to **weekly tracking**. Every Sunday, she would sit down with her bank statement and categorize her spending for the week. This gave her enough perspective to see patterns without feeling like she was obsessing over every dollar.

Finally, Sarah experimented with **monthly tracking**. At the end of the month, she would look at her total spending and compare it to her budget. This gave her a big-picture view — but it didn't give her enough time to adjust her behavior during the month.

Eventually, Sarah found that a combination of weekly and monthly tracking worked best for her.

She would track her spending weekly to make adjustments in real-time — but she would also review her spending monthly to measure progress and fine-tune her budget. This balance helped her stay on track without feeling overwhelmed.

Tracking your spending is like stepping on the scale when you're trying to lose weight. Daily tracking can feel obsessive — but if you only weigh yourself once a month, you might not catch small problems before they spiral out of control. Weekly tracking gives you enough feedback to adjust your habits while still seeing the bigger picture.

Apps and Tools to Help Monitor Spending

Sarah knew that tracking her spending manually was helpful — but also time-consuming. She wanted to find a way to automate the process without losing the awareness that comes from seeing where her money was going.

That's when she started experimenting with different budgeting apps and tools.

Her first stop was **Mint** — one of the most popular budgeting apps. Mint automatically linked to her bank accounts and categorized her expenses. Sarah liked that Mint gave her a real-time overview of her spending — but she found the notifications overwhelming. She would get alerts about going over budget in specific categories, which made her feel guilty rather than motivated.

Next, Sarah tried **YNAB (You Need a Budget)**. YNAB focused more on giving every dollar a "job" — meaning she had to actively decide where to put her money at the beginning of each month. Sarah found that YNAB helped her feel more in control — but the setup process was complicated, and she struggled to stay consistent.

Finally, Sarah landed on **PocketGuard** — an app that showed her how much "spendable" money she had left after covering her essential expenses. PocketGuard's simple interface worked well for Sarah because it focused on what she *could* spend rather than what she *couldn't* spend. This gave her a feeling of freedom instead of restriction.

Sarah realized that there's no one-size-fits-all solution when it comes to tracking apps. Some people thrive on detailed data (which makes Mint and YNAB great options), while others need a simplified, high-level overview (which makes PocketGuard or Clarity Money more appealing).

The key is to choose an app that matches your personality and spending style. Sarah's goal wasn't to track every penny — it was to stay aware of her spending without feeling like she was constantly under surveillance.

Sarah ultimately decided to use PocketGuard for daily tracking and YNAB for big-picture monthly tracking. This combination allowed her to see both the short-term and long-term impact of her spending — without getting bogged down in details.

Manual vs. Automated Tracking

Sarah also had to figure out whether she preferred manual or automated tracking.

When you track your spending manually — by writing down expenses or entering them into a spreadsheet — you create a high level of awareness. You feel every purchase because you have to physically record it.

On the other hand, automated tracking (through bank apps or budgeting software) saves time and gives you a broader perspective. But it can also make you feel disconnected from your spending because the app does the work for you.

Sarah started with manual tracking to get a better sense of her habits. For the first month, she kept a spending journal where she wrote down every dollar she spent — even the small purchases like coffee and snacks.

This process was eye-opening. Sarah hadn't realized how much she was spending on takeout and impulse shopping until she saw the totals on paper.

After that first month, Sarah switched to automated tracking. She linked her bank accounts to PocketGuard and

YNAB, which allowed her to categorize expenses automatically and track her overall spending trends.

The combination of manual and automated tracking worked well for Sarah. The manual tracking phase helped her reset her spending habits, while the automated tracking phase allowed her to save time and stay consistent.

Sarah also developed a simple habit: anytime she felt tempted to buy something impulsively, she would check her budgeting app first. Seeing how much money she had left for "fun spending" helped her avoid overspending — without feeling guilty.

Bringing It All Together

After three months of consistent tracking, Sarah had a clear understanding of her financial reality — and that changed everything.

She discovered that she was spending an average of **$250 a month** on takeout and an additional **$150** on impulse shopping. By cutting her takeout spending in half and setting a $50 monthly limit on shopping, she was able to save an extra **$200 a month** — which she redirected toward debt repayment and building her emergency fund.

Tracking also gave Sarah the confidence to adjust her budget when needed. If she had an expensive month (like when her car needed repairs), she didn't panic — she simply adjusted her spending the following month to balance things out.

Sarah's biggest realization was that tracking her spending wasn't about punishment — it was about empowerment. By knowing where her money was going, she was able to make better decisions, avoid wasteful spending, and build the financial security she had always wanted.

Budgeting is about more than just numbers — it's about creating a system that works for *you*. Sarah learned that when you track your spending consistently and honestly, you take control of your finances — and that's when real change starts to happen.

Section 2.3: Sticking to the Budget

Sarah had been here before.

She'd started budgets more times than she could count — downloaded the apps, created the spreadsheets, and promised herself that *this time* would be different. But somehow, it always fell apart.

The first couple of weeks were usually fine. She'd track her spending carefully, cut back on takeout, and feel proud of herself when she resisted the urge to buy something unnecessary. But then something would happen.

Maybe it was a stressful week at work. Maybe her friends invited her out for drinks, and she didn't want to say no. Maybe she just got tired of feeling restricted.

Whatever the reason, Sarah would end up overspending — and then the guilt would kick in. "I'm bad with money," she'd think. "I'll never figure this out."

Then she'd abandon the budget altogether.

This time, though, Sarah was determined to make it stick. She had finally created a minimalist budget that made sense. She had separated her needs from her wants, automated her savings, and cut back on unnecessary expenses.

The next challenge wasn't *building* the budget — it was *sticking to it.*

Sticking to a budget isn't about discipline or self-control — it's about creating a system that supports you when things get hard. You need accountability, flexibility, and motivation to keep going when the initial excitement wears off.

Sarah realized that if she wanted to stay on track, she needed to find a way to stay consistent without feeling deprived — and that meant building accountability, managing budgeting fatigue, and learning how to reward herself without blowing up her progress.

Building Accountability

Sarah knew she needed help.

In the past, she had always tried to manage her finances in isolation. She didn't want to talk to her friends about money because it felt personal — and frankly, a little embarrassing.

But when Sarah read about the power of accountability, she decided to give it a try. She reached out to her friend Emily, who had always been good with money, and asked if they could start a "money check-in" once a month.

At first, it felt awkward. Sarah wasn't used to talking about money openly — and admitting that she had a problem sticking to her budget made her feel vulnerable. But Emily was supportive. She didn't judge Sarah for her past mistakes — instead, she helped her brainstorm solutions.

They decided to meet once a month over coffee and review their budgets together. Sarah would bring her bank statement and talk through how well she had stuck to her plan. Emily would offer advice, but more importantly, she would listen.

Having someone else involved made a huge difference. Knowing that she had to sit down with Emily every month made Sarah more thoughtful about her spending decisions.

When she felt the urge to splurge on clothes or order takeout, she would ask herself, *"How will I explain this to Emily?"* That extra moment of hesitation was often enough to help her make better choices.

Sarah also joined an online budgeting group where people shared their wins and setbacks. Seeing other people struggle and succeed made her feel less alone. She realized that budgeting wasn't about being perfect — it was about making progress.

Accountability doesn't mean handing over control of your money to someone else — it means creating a support system that helps you stay focused. Whether it's a friend, a family member, or an online community, having someone to check in with makes it easier to stick to your goals.

Overcoming Budgeting Fatigue

By the third month, Sarah hit a wall.

At first, budgeting had felt empowering. She loved watching her savings grow and seeing her debt balance shrink. But after a few months, the excitement started to fade.

She was tired of tracking every expense. Tired of saying "no" to things she wanted. Tired of feeling like every spending decision was a test.

Sarah was experiencing **budgeting fatigue** — the feeling of mental exhaustion that comes from constantly monitoring and managing your money.

She knew she had to find a way to keep going — because quitting now would undo all the progress she had made.

The first thing Sarah did was take a break from tracking.

For one week, she gave herself permission to step back. She didn't abandon her budget entirely — she just stopped logging every single expense. She allowed herself to spend a little more freely — but within reason.

At the end of the week, Sarah felt refreshed. The break reminded her that budgeting wasn't about punishment — it was about building a sustainable system that worked for *her*.

Next, she simplified her budget.

At the beginning of her budgeting journey, Sarah had created multiple spending categories — groceries, gas, entertainment, personal care, and so on. Now, she consolidated everything into three categories:

- **Essentials** (rent, utilities, groceries, and transportation)
- **Savings** (emergency fund and debt repayment)
- **Fun Money** (everything else)

This made tracking easier — and it gave Sarah more flexibility. If she spent more on groceries one week, she didn't feel like a failure — she just adjusted her fun money or savings contribution to balance it out.

Sarah also stopped trying to be perfect. If she went over her budget one week, she didn't punish herself — she adjusted. If she had a more expensive month because of car repairs or a birthday, she rolled with it.

Budgeting isn't about perfection — it's about consistency. Sarah realized that she could have an "off" month without losing all of her progress.

Rewarding Progress Without Overspending

One of the reasons Sarah had failed in the past was because she felt deprived.

Cutting back on spending and paying off debt felt responsible — but it also felt boring. After a few months, Sarah would get frustrated and splurge as a way of rebelling against her own budget.

This time, she built in rewards from the beginning.

Sarah decided to create a **milestone reward system**. Every time she reached a savings or debt repayment milestone, she would treat herself — but within reason.

After she saved her first $500, Sarah allowed herself to buy a new pair of shoes she'd been eyeing. When she paid off her first credit card, she booked a massage.

The key was that these rewards were planned — not impulsive. Sarah set aside a small "reward fund" each month, so the money for her treats didn't come from her essential budget or savings.

She also created non-monetary rewards.

When Sarah reached a budgeting milestone, she would give herself a "free day" — a day where she didn't have to track expenses or think about money. Sometimes she would spend the day binge-watching TV or going for a long hike with friends.

These rewards kept Sarah motivated. They reminded her that budgeting wasn't about sacrifice — it was about building a life she enjoyed.

Sarah also found joy in tracking her progress. She created a visual savings chart where she colored in sections every time she hit a milestone. Seeing the chart fill up gave her a sense of accomplishment and kept her motivated to keep going.

The more Sarah rewarded herself in healthy, balanced ways, the less tempted she felt to blow up her budget with impulsive spending.

Bringing It All Together

After six months of sticking to her minimalist budget, Sarah had paid off $1,200 of credit card debt, built a $2,000 emergency fund, and had enough savings set aside to book a vacation.

The difference this time wasn't the budget itself — it was how Sarah stayed committed to it.

By building accountability with her friend Emily and her online group, Sarah had created a support system that helped her stay focused. By adjusting her budget when fatigue set in, she learned to adapt instead of quitting. And by rewarding herself in small, intentional ways, Sarah stayed motivated without undoing her progress.

Sticking to a budget isn't about self-control — it's about building a system that supports you when things get hard.

Sarah's story proves that when you create a budget that's realistic, flexible, and rewarding — sticking to it becomes easier than you ever imagined.

Chapter 3

Cutting Expenses Without Sacrificing Quality of Life

Section 3.1: Reducing Fixed Expenses

Sarah used to think that cutting expenses meant giving things up.

To her, budgeting had always sounded like a list of "no's" — no dining out, no streaming services, no fun. But once she started getting serious about her finances, she realized that not all expense-cutting had to be painful. In fact, one of the biggest wins came not from cutting out life's joys, but from lowering the costs of things she already needed — her fixed expenses.

These were the non-negotiables: rent, utilities, phone bill, car insurance. They showed up like clockwork every month and took up a huge portion of her paycheck. Sarah had always assumed there wasn't much she could do about them. After all, fixed meant *fixed*, right?

But she was wrong.

Reducing fixed expenses didn't mean she had to move to a cheaper city or sell her car overnight. It just required a little research, a few phone calls, and the willingness to ask for better deals. What surprised her most was how quickly these small changes added up — without requiring her to sacrifice her quality of life.

It started with her **rent**. Sarah lived in a decent apartment in a building she liked, but when her lease renewal notice arrived with a $75 monthly increase, she panicked. She didn't want to move — but she also couldn't justify the bump.

Instead of quietly accepting it, she reached out to her landlord.

She was nervous, but she approached the conversation with preparation. She mentioned her on-time payment record, her good standing as a tenant, and the current market trends — she had done her homework and found that similar units in the area hadn't increased rent by more than $25.

To her surprise, the landlord agreed to reduce the proposed increase from $75 to just $20. It wasn't a huge win on paper, but it saved her **$660 a year** — just for speaking up.

That experience gave Sarah the confidence to look for other ways to lower her recurring bills. She started with her **internet provider**, where she was paying $90 a month for a plan she rarely used to its full potential. One phone call and a bit of polite persistence got her a promotional rate of $60 — and they even increased her speed.

Next came her **cell phone plan**. Sarah had been paying $80 a month for unlimited data, but when she checked her usage, she found she rarely used more than 5GB. She downgraded her plan and brought her bill down to $45 a month.

The lesson was clear: companies often charge more because people are willing to pay more — not because the higher price is necessary.

Sarah then turned her attention to **subscriptions**.

She was spending $75 a month on services that, individually, didn't seem like a big deal. Netflix, Hulu, Spotify, a fitness app, a meditation app, cloud storage, and a couple of online magazines she forgot she even subscribed to.

When she saw the total all together, she was shocked.

It wasn't that Sarah didn't enjoy these services — it's that she didn't enjoy *all of them*. She couldn't remember the last time she opened Hulu, and the meditation app had been used only twice since she downloaded it.

Rather than canceling everything outright, Sarah decided to prioritize. She picked two services she actually used and looked forward to — Netflix and Spotify — and paused or canceled the rest.

She also found that many subscription services offer seasonal discounts or pause options. Instead of paying $10 monthly for her fitness app, she opted for a $60 annual plan that cut the cost in half.

In total, Sarah shaved off nearly $40 a month from subscriptions — a number that felt small day to day, but added up to **almost $500 a year**.

And she didn't feel deprived at all. If anything, she appreciated the few services she kept even more.

The final piece of Sarah's fixed expense puzzle was **insurance**.

Insurance was one of those things she never thought much about. She paid her car insurance, renter's insurance, and health premiums without question, assuming there wasn't much wiggle room.

But on a whim — motivated by a budgeting podcast she'd been listening to — Sarah decided to shop around for a better car insurance rate.

She called three other companies and got quotes. To her surprise, one of them offered the exact same coverage for **$35 less per month**. When she called her current provider and told them about the quote, they offered to match it.

All it took was an hour of phone calls to save **$420 a year**.

Sarah then asked her provider about additional discounts — things like bundling renters and car insurance, safe driver rewards, and even discounts for setting up auto-pay. With those changes, she saved another $10 a month.

What made this journey so powerful wasn't just the money saved — it was the mindset shift.

Sarah had always believed that financial improvement required big sacrifices. But what she discovered was that just a few phone calls, a little negotiation, and the willingness to be intentional with her recurring expenses gave her hundreds of dollars in breathing room every month.

She didn't give up her home, her phone, or her favorite shows. She just paid *less* for the same life — and that's what cutting fixed expenses is really about.

It's not about making your life smaller — it's about making your money stretch further, so you can invest in what truly matters.

By the end of the month, Sarah had saved more than $150 in recurring costs — money she immediately redirected toward building her emergency fund and paying off debt. And she felt empowered, not restricted.

She wasn't surviving anymore — she was choosing. And that choice made all the difference.

Section 3.2: Saving on Food and Essentials

It was a Saturday morning when Sarah found herself staring at her grocery receipt in the parking lot, stunned at the total.

She hadn't bought anything extravagant — just a few meals for the week, some snacks, and the usual household items. Yet somehow, the bill had crossed $150. Again.

The frustrating part wasn't just the amount — it was how quickly that food seemed to disappear. By midweek, she'd be ordering takeout again, claiming she had "nothing to eat" at home.

This was one of those expenses that crept up quietly. It wasn't flashy or indulgent. It didn't feel irresponsible. But when Sarah sat down and reviewed her monthly spending, food and household essentials were taking up nearly as much of her budget as rent.

She knew she had to make a change — but she didn't want to live on ramen or coupon clip for hours every week.

What she discovered was that saving money on food and essentials didn't have to mean cutting back on quality or flavor. It was about being intentional, staying one step ahead of her cravings, and learning a few tricks that made a big difference over time.

The turning point came when Sarah started **planning her meals**.

Up until then, her grocery shopping had been impulsive. She'd walk into the store with a vague idea of what she wanted and fill her cart based on cravings and guesses. A pack of chicken, some frozen meals, three types of cheese, two different sauces — with no real plan for how they'd come together.

Then, halfway through the week, she'd realize she was out of key ingredients or tired of what she'd bought, and she'd reach for the takeout app.

So, one Sunday, Sarah sat down with a notepad and decided to map out her week. She chose five meals she liked — nothing fancy, just things she knew she'd actually eat. She made a list of all the ingredients she needed, double-checked what she already had at home, and headed to the store with a plan.

That week, her grocery bill came to $92 — nearly $60 less than the week before — and she didn't order takeout once.

The magic wasn't in deprivation; it was in intention.

Meal planning gave Sarah structure, but she wanted to go a step further. She started **batch cooking** on Sundays. She'd roast a tray of vegetables, cook a big pot of rice, and prep proteins like chicken or ground turkey in bulk.

These ingredients became mix-and-match meals throughout the week: tacos one night, a grain bowl the next and stir fry the day after.

Batch cooking saved her time during the week and made it easier to resist the urge to order out when she was tired.

Knowing there was already something cooked in the fridge — something she actually liked — made all the difference.

Even breakfast became easier. Instead of grabbing a $4 latte and $3 pastry on her way to work, Sarah prepped overnight oats and brought coffee from home.

That one change saved her nearly $30 a week — over $100 a month — without making her feel like she was missing out.

Another eye-opener for Sarah was how much **strategic shopping** could save her without changing what she ate.

Before, she'd shop at the same store out of habit, assuming all prices were more or less the same. But when she started comparing prices — even between locations of the same chain — she saw stark differences.

She began rotating between two grocery stores depending on the week's needs. One had better produce prices, while the other had sales on household essentials and pantry staples.

She also stopped ignoring store brands. At first, Sarah hesitated to switch from name-brand products — but when she finally tried the store-brand almond milk, paper towels, and cereal, she couldn't tell the difference. What she *could* see was the price: 20 to 30 percent lower for nearly identical items.

Over time, Sarah also got smarter about **finding deals**.

She signed up for her grocery store's loyalty program and started checking the weekly flyer online before shopping. This helped her build her meals around what was on sale instead of shopping first and figuring out deals later.

She didn't spend hours coupon clipping like her grandmother used to — instead, she used a couple of apps on her phone.

One was a digital coupon app from her grocery chain. The other was a cashback app that gave her small rebates for things she was already buying, like yogurt or laundry detergent. She'd snap a quick picture of her receipt and get $1 or $2 back here and there. It wasn't much, but it added up.

After a few months, she cashed out the app and used the money to treat herself to a nice dinner out — guilt-free.

Sarah also applied the same thinking to non-food essentials.

She stopped buying cleaning products individually and instead bought a few items in bulk at a discount store. She switched to reusable cleaning cloths instead of paper towels. She kept an eye out for "buy one, get one" deals on toothpaste and shampoo.

None of these changes made her feel like she was sacrificing anything — in fact, she liked the feeling of being stocked up and prepared.

By focusing on **efficiency over excess**, she realized how much money she had been wasting out of habit or convenience.

The biggest shift, though, was psychological.

Saving money on food and essentials didn't mean eating worse or living without — it meant being more mindful. Sarah began to enjoy the process of planning meals, cooking at home, and even spotting deals. It became a form of self-care.

She still treated herself now and then — a latte from her favorite café, a dinner out with friends — but those moments felt special instead of routine. They were choices, not defaults.

By the end of her first three months of mindful grocery shopping, batch cooking, and deal-hunting, Sarah had saved more than **$400** on food and essentials — all without giving up the foods she loved or drastically changing her lifestyle.

She no longer dreaded checking her bank account or feeling that post-grocery guilt. She felt empowered, resourceful, and in control.

Cutting expenses doesn't have to be about doing less — sometimes it's about doing things *smarter*. And when you approach your food and essentials with intention instead of autopilot, you may find you're not only saving money — you're actually living better.

Section 3.3: Saving on Entertainment and Extras

For Sarah, weekends used to mean spending money.

Dinner with friends, a movie, maybe brunch the next day. A spontaneous shopping trip or a concert ticket "just because." It wasn't that she was trying to live lavishly — it just felt like the only way to enjoy her time off. But when she started taking a hard look at her finances, she realized her entertainment spending was draining her budget faster than anything else.

Still, she hesitated to cut back.

Life already felt serious enough — working long hours, managing bills, paying off debt. The idea of giving up the little joys, the fun moments, the social outings? It felt depressing.

But as Sarah soon discovered, *cutting back on entertainment didn't have to mean cutting out fun*. It was simply about finding new ways to enjoy herself — ways that didn't come with a hefty price tag.

It started with a walk.

One sunny afternoon, feeling restless but not wanting to spend, Sarah headed to a nearby park with her journal and a podcast queued up on her phone. She sat on a bench for an hour, watched people walk their dogs, sipped the coffee she brought from home, and felt something she hadn't in a while — peaceful.

That moment sparked a realization: the feeling she was chasing through expensive entertainment wasn't always about the event — it was about connection, relaxation, stimulation, joy. And those feelings could come from more than just spending money.

Sarah began exploring local free events — something she'd always overlooked before. Her city's website listed free outdoor movie nights, museum days, and weekend farmer's markets. The public library had author talks and book clubs. The community center offered free yoga once a week.

Instead of automatically reaching for her wallet to find fun, she started looking for what was already available.

One Friday, she invited a couple of friends over for a "build your own taco night" and movie marathon. They brought toppings, she made the tortillas, and they streamed a few feel-good movies on her couch. It cost a fraction of what a night out would have — and no one missed the restaurant noise or the expensive cocktails.

The shift in her mindset grew stronger when she finally made the decision to **cancel her cable subscription**.

She had been paying $110 a month for a package she barely used. She watched maybe five channels regularly — most of which were available through streaming. So, she made the leap: canceled cable, returned the bulky box, and signed up for one streaming service at $10 a month.

The change saved her $1,200 a year.

At first, she thought she'd miss having hundreds of channels. But instead, she found she watched more intentionally — choosing shows and movies she actually wanted to see, rather than flipping through channels out of boredom.

Streaming also allowed her to pause subscriptions she wasn't using. She could rotate between services each month instead of subscribing to all of them at once. One month she had Netflix, the next month it might be Hulu. This kept her entertainment fresh — and her spending lean.

But perhaps the most important shift came in how Sarah approached *socializing.*

Before, hanging out with friends almost always meant spending money — going out to eat, grabbing drinks, or heading to events with pricey tickets. It didn't feel like there were alternatives, and saying "no" often felt like missing out.

But after she opened up to a few close friends about her budgeting goals, something unexpected happened.

They got it.

Many of them were dealing with the same financial stress but hadn't said anything either. Together, they got creative.

Instead of going out to dinner, they started hosting potlucks where each person brought a dish. They had themed nights — pasta night, game night, even a "cook something you've never made before" challenge.

They went on group hikes, explored free museums, and attended community festivals. One friend found a local trivia night with no cover charge — and it became a weekly tradition.

These new routines didn't just save money — they brought everyone closer. There was something more personal and relaxed about gathering at someone's home or walking through a park together than shouting across a noisy restaurant table.

And because no one was trying to impress or compete, the pressure to spend disappeared.

Sarah didn't stop doing things she loved — she just stopped letting a price tag dictate her happiness.

Now, when she wanted to go out for a concert or a big night, she planned for it. She made it intentional — not routine. And because it wasn't happening all the time, it felt more special.

What used to be casual, costly habits became thoughtful, budget-friendly choices.

She even created a "fun fund" — a small portion of her monthly budget that she set aside just for experiences. Some months, she barely touched it because she had so many free options. Other months, she'd use it for a play or dinner out.

But the difference was that she was in control.

By making entertainment a conscious part of her budget — rather than an automatic expense — Sarah was able to cut hundreds from her monthly spending without feeling like she was missing out.

She had more free time, stronger relationships, and a deeper sense of joy in her day-to-day life — all because she learned how to enjoy herself without overspending.

And in the end, she realized something important: the best memories don't always come with a receipt.

Chapter 4

Increasing Your Income

Section 4.1: Side Hustles and Gig Work

Sarah was tired of the math not adding up.

She had trimmed her budget, cut back on takeout, canceled subscriptions she barely used, and switched to generic brands at the grocery store. Still, even after all the effort, her savings grew slowly, and the idea of paying off her student loans felt like chasing the horizon — always out of reach.

One afternoon, as she reviewed her budget, a thought crossed her mind: *Maybe I don't just need to spend less — maybe I need to earn more.*

The idea of a side hustle had always been in the back of her mind, but she hadn't taken it seriously. She assumed it meant starting a business, investing money she didn't have, or working every free hour she could find. And with a full-time job already consuming most of her energy, she wasn't sure she had it in her.

But when she dug a little deeper, Sarah discovered that the world of gig work and side income wasn't one-size-fits-all. It wasn't about burning out or chasing passive income dreams that never quite materialized — it was about using her existing skills and time creatively to generate a little extra breathing room.

Sarah began by making a list — not of jobs, but of *what she was good at.*

She was a solid writer, had a knack for organization, and people always complimented her on her calm demeanor and ability to explain things clearly. She'd helped friends clean out closets, edit their resumes, and even babysit on weekends. None of these things felt like "work" at the time — but now, looking at them with a new lens, she saw potential.

Within a week, Sarah had created a profile on a freelance site offering resume editing and cover letter writing. She also signed up for a local babysitting network and posted in a neighborhood group about helping with weekend decluttering sessions or garage sales.

Her first gig came from a former coworker who needed help updating their LinkedIn profile. Sarah charged $40, and the project took her less than two hours. Not only was it easy — it felt good. It was energizing to know that her skills were valuable to someone else and even better to know that money could be earned outside the 9-to-5.

She followed that project with a couple more — helping someone write an apartment application letter, tutoring a teenager in English, and eventually picking up a few paid writing gigs online. It wasn't consistent, but it didn't need to be. Even an extra $200 a month made a noticeable difference.

At first, she worried that balancing a side hustle with her full-time job would wear her down. But she quickly realized that the secret wasn't to do *more*, it was to do it *smarter.*

Sarah made a rule: she would only take on side gigs that aligned with three criteria — low prep, flexible hours and personal enjoyment. If something felt like a burden before she even started, it didn't make the cut.

This meant that she turned down some higher-paying gigs that came with unrealistic expectations or tight deadlines. She never worked more than 10 hours a week on side projects — usually closer to five.

What helped her maintain this balance was learning to treat her side hustle like a partner, not a boss. It was there to *support* her goals, not control her life. She carved out set "side hustle hours" during the week — often Saturday mornings and a couple evenings a week — and stuck to them. This gave her structure without feeling overwhelmed.

Still, there were moments when fatigue crept in.

One particularly exhausting week, Sarah had taken on two writing gigs on top of her full-time job, and by Friday, she felt like she'd hit a wall. She was mentally drained and couldn't even enjoy the $300 she'd earned — it felt like she'd traded too much of herself for it.

That was when she recognized the early signs of **burnout** — and decided to make a change.

She learned that burnout didn't always look dramatic. Sometimes, it was subtle: irritation at small tasks, the dread of opening emails, or struggling to focus on simple things. It often crept in when she said "yes" too often or tied her self-worth to constant productivity.

So, she hit pause. She took a week off from all side gigs, no matter how tempting the offers. She went on walks, spent time with friends, and watched movies without checking her email.

When she came back, she restructured her schedule with breathing room built in. She added a "no hustle" rule for Sundays and gave herself the freedom to decline work without guilt. The goal wasn't to make extra money at the cost of her sanity — it was to create freedom, not stress.

The most surprising thing? Even with these boundaries, her side income grew.

Because she was more focused and energized, her work was better — and clients referred her to others. She raised her rates slightly, narrowed her offerings to only what she enjoyed most, and found that she could make the same money in fewer hours.

Sarah also discovered that gig work could be seasonal. Some months were busier than others, and that was okay. She used slower months to rest, learn new skills, or dream up new offerings.

Eventually, her side hustle became more than a financial tool — it became a creative outlet. It reminded her of her talents, gave her confidence, and allowed her to take pressure off her day job without jumping into the unknown.

She didn't have to launch a business or hustle 24/7. She just had to start where she was, with what she had.

The real win wasn't just the extra money — though that helped her pay off a credit card and start a vacation fund. The real win was the feeling of empowerment.

She no longer felt stuck, waiting for a raise or a windfall. She had built a small but steady stream of income that she controlled — on her terms, with her time.

And as it turns out, sometimes the best way to stretch your budget isn't to cut more — it's to *create more.*

Sarah learned that increasing your income doesn't have to mean sacrificing your peace. With the right mindset, a little strategy and clear boundaries, a side hustle can be a source of possibility — not pressure.

Section 4.2: Negotiating a Raise or Promotion

Sarah had been working at her job for almost three years. She liked the team, was good at what she did, and had taken on more responsibilities than when she first started. What hadn't changed much, though, was her paycheck.

Every month, as she updated her budget and strategized how to stretch her income, the same thought kept bubbling up: *I deserve more than this.*

But when it came to actually asking for a raise, she froze.

It wasn't that she didn't believe in her value — deep down, she knew she was contributing. But the idea of walking into her boss's office, making her case, and potentially hearing "no" made her stomach turn.

She worried about seeming ungrateful or coming across as demanding. What if her boss thought she was replaceable? What if asking for more actually backfired?

Still, the alternative — staying silent and hoping someone noticed her hard work — hadn't gotten her anywhere. If she wanted to grow her income, she had to learn how to advocate for herself.

So, she made a plan.

Sarah started by observing the rhythm of her company. She paid attention to when annual reviews happened and how promotions were typically handled. When she noticed that performance reviews were scheduled for the end of the quarter, she gave herself two months to prepare.

That time wasn't just for mustering courage — it was for gathering evidence.

She started keeping a private document on her computer called her "Wins List." Every time she completed a project, received praise from a client or manager, helped improve a process, or took on something outside her original role, she documented it.

It felt awkward at first — like she was bragging to herself. But over time, that list became a reminder of her impact, especially on days when she doubted her progress.

When review season approached, Sarah scheduled a one-on-one with her manager. She didn't wait for the subject of raises to come up on its own — she initiated the conversation with intention.

She started by expressing her appreciation for the opportunities she'd had on the team and framed the conversation around growth: both hers and the company's. She shared specific examples of projects she had taken on, the results she had delivered, and the ways she had gone beyond her job description.

Then, she asked: *"Based on my contributions and the market rate for this role, I'd like to discuss a salary adjustment that reflects the value I'm bringing to the team."*

Her tone was confident, but respectful. It wasn't an ultimatum — it was a conversation.

She had done her homework too. Sarah had looked up salary benchmarks for her role using sites like Glassdoor and Payscale, and she was prepared to share those if needed — though she didn't lead with them. She focused on her **value**, not just market rates.

Her manager listened. He didn't say yes right away — but he didn't say no either. He asked a few follow-up questions, took notes, and promised to bring it up with leadership.

The wait that followed was nerve-wracking. For two weeks, Sarah checked her inbox constantly, wondering if she'd pushed too hard. But then, she got the news: a **7% salary increase**, effective the next pay period.

It wasn't everything she hoped for, but it was a clear step forward. More importantly, it was proof that asking for what she deserved could *work*.

Not every ask leads to an immediate "yes," and Sarah knew that.

She'd had a different experience a year earlier at a previous job. Back then, she had gathered her courage, asked for a raise — and was told flatly that "it wasn't in the budget."

At the time, it stung.

She had walked into the conversation with hope and walked out feeling deflated. But over time, she realized that how she responded to that "no" mattered just as much as the conversation itself.

Instead of shutting down, she responded professionally. She thanked her manager for the conversation, asked for feedback on areas she could grow in and requested a timeline for when a raise might be possible.

That move changed everything.

While the raise never came at that company — she ended up leaving six months later for a better-paying opportunity — her calm, measured response maintained her professional reputation. And she walked into her next job interview with a stronger sense of what she was worth.

Sometimes, "no" just means "not yet." And sometimes, it's a sign that you've outgrown where you are.

Either way, Sarah learned not to fear the conversation.

Over time, she started coaching friends through their own negotiations. What she told them, again and again, was this: **you are your best advocate**.

Managers aren't mind-readers. They're juggling dozens of priorities, and even well-meaning ones may not notice everything you're doing unless you show them.

Advocating for a raise isn't about arrogance — it's about alignment. It's about connecting the value you bring to the outcomes your employer cares about and making a case that's hard to ignore.

And when you do it well — when you prepare, speak with clarity and handle the outcome professionally — you come out stronger, no matter what the answer is.

Sarah's confidence didn't come from getting everything she asked for — it came from knowing she had the tools to ask in the first place.

She no longer waited for recognition. She created it.

And once she saw what was possible, she never went back to hoping for more. She learned to *ask* — and that single shift made a lasting difference in her financial life.

Section 4.3: Selling Unused Items and Passive Income

When Sarah opened her hall closet one Saturday afternoon, she wasn't planning to make money — she was just trying to find her winter boots.

But as she dug through bins of forgotten shoes, an old yoga mat, some barely-used kitchen gadgets, and a pile of clothes she hadn't worn in years, a thought struck her: *Why am I hanging on to all this stuff?*

Most of it was still in great shape. A few pieces even had tags. She'd held onto them out of habit or the idea that she "might use them someday," but deep down, she knew that wasn't going to happen.

That's when a light bulb went off: maybe these unused things could become the stepping stone to something bigger — extra income, a clearer space, and a lighter mental load.

She started with the easiest stuff: clothes. A pair of boots she'd only worn once, a jacket she'd outgrown, a few dresses that didn't suit her style anymore. She snapped photos, wrote simple but honest descriptions, and listed them on a local resale app. Within two days, she'd made $85.

It wasn't just the money that excited her — it was the feeling of turning clutter into cash.

Next, she posted a small bookshelf, an old coffee maker, and a lamp that no longer matched her decor. The messages started coming in. Some haggled, some didn't. By the end of the week, she'd made over $300 — and her apartment felt noticeably cleaner.

What surprised Sarah most was how many platforms made selling simple. Facebook Marketplace was ideal for local items, especially furniture and home goods. Poshmark worked well for clothing, and OfferUp was a go-to for odd household items. Even eBay became a playground for niche things she hadn't thought were worth much — like an old iPod and a vintage camera her uncle had given her.

The process snowballed. Every drawer and shelf in her home became a new opportunity.

Of course, she had to be careful. A few people tried to lowball her to ridiculous levels, and one person didn't show up after agreeing to buy a dresser. But she learned to vet buyers, stick to local pickup and never meet someone alone.

Through it all, Sarah realized that *decluttering had become a side hustle.*

Once the bigger items were gone, she got more strategic. She even helped a friend clean out their garage and split the profits from what they sold. It became more than just about making money — it was about freeing herself from "stuff" that no longer served her.

But after a few months, the pile of things to sell began to shrink. That's when Sarah turned her attention to something she'd been hearing about for years but never taken seriously: *passive income.*

To her, passive income had always sounded like a fantasy — something only rich people could access or entrepreneurs with large followings. But the more she read, the more she realized that passive income wasn't always glamorous or instant — sometimes, it was just about creating something once and letting it slowly build value.

She started small.

Sarah had written a few short guides for friends about resume writing and job hunting — now, she turned them into a downloadable PDF and listed it on Etsy for $5. It took her one afternoon to design it and a few days to promote it through her social media and a career-focused Facebook group.

Within the first month, she made $40. Not much, but it came in while she was sleeping.

Encouraged, she explored other ideas.

She created a few digital planners and budgeting templates using free design software, then uploaded them to an online marketplace. Some sold, some didn't. But with each product, she learned more — how to market it better, how to use keywords, what people actually wanted.

None of this made her rich overnight. But over time, these tiny trickles of income started adding up. One week it was $15, the next $70. It wasn't about hitting it big — it was about building small streams that supported her larger goals.

Of course, not everything was smooth sailing.

Once, Sarah came across a "passive income course" promising to teach her how to make thousands a month by flipping digital products. The website looked flashy and the testimonials sounded compelling. But when she dug deeper, there were red flags — vague guarantees, no clear creator info and lots of upsells.

She almost paid the $297 course fee before something in her gut told her to pause. Instead, she researched reviews from outside sources and found several posts warning about the program's shady practices.

It was a wake-up call.

Not every opportunity was worth chasing. And in the world of passive income, *if it sounds too good to be true — it probably is.*

Sarah learned to avoid anyone selling a dream without a clear, practical path. She focused on what she could control: things she could create, sell, or share based on her real skills and interests.

Instead of jumping into crypto schemes or investing in courses with no guarantee of results, she leaned into authenticity. Her passive income wasn't flashy, but it was real.

She also made a promise to herself: before spending money on any "income opportunity," she'd ask three questions:

1. Do I understand how it works?
2. Can I afford to lose this money if it fails?
3. Does it align with my skills or values?

That approach helped her stay grounded, especially in a world full of online promises.

By the end of six months, Sarah had sold over $1,000 worth of items, built a small but steady flow of income from digital products, and avoided throwing money at empty promises.

She wasn't just earning more — she was reclaiming her time, her space and her confidence.

And perhaps most importantly, she no longer felt helpless when it came to her income. She had learned that money doesn't only come from your day job. Sometimes it's sitting in your closet. Sometimes it's hidden in a skill you've overlooked. Sometimes, it's waiting to be built — one small step at a time.

Chapter 5

Dealing with Debt

Section 5.1: Understanding Your Debt

Sarah used to avoid her mailbox. Every time she opened it, there was a new reminder of a financial decision she'd rather forget — a credit card statement, a student loan update, a medical bill she'd been ignoring. Each envelope represented a different kind of stress, and together they created a quiet, constant weight on her shoulders.

At first, she tried not to think about it. She made minimum payments here and there, shuffled balances around when she could, and told herself that as long as she wasn't in collections, she was "managing" her debt. But the truth was, she didn't actually know how much she owed.

And that lack of clarity kept her stuck.

It wasn't until she sat down one night, frustrated after another paycheck had vanished into a dozen small payments, that Sarah decided something had to change. She opened her laptop, grabbed a notebook, and — heart racing — pulled up every debt she could think of.

Credit cards. Student loans. A lingering hospital bill. A financing plan for her old laptop.

Seeing the full list in one place was overwhelming at first. But then something unexpected happened. As the picture came into focus, so did her sense of control.

She had five separate debts, spread across different lenders. Some had small balances under $500, others were several thousand dollars. What varied even more were the interest rates — one credit card was charging her nearly 26% interest. Another was closer to 18%. Her student loans were in the 6% range, and the medical bill had no interest but a looming due date.

Sarah realized she had been treating all her debts the same — tossing a bit of money at each and hoping it would all somehow work out. But by doing that, she was making very little progress. She was stuck on a treadmill, running hard but getting nowhere.

The turning point came when she learned how interest rates really worked.

She'd known, in theory, that higher interest meant higher costs. But when she used a debt calculator online to estimate how much her 26% APR credit card would cost if she kept paying only the minimum, the result made her stomach flip. That one card — with a balance of $2,000 — would end up costing her over $4,000 and take *years* to pay off if she kept doing what she was doing.

That's when it clicked: she needed a strategy, not just effort.

Sarah organized her list not just by balance, but by interest rate. Suddenly, it was obvious where her focus needed to be. That high-interest credit card wasn't just annoying — it was an emergency. Every month, she carried a balance and the cost was snowballing.

Instead of panicking, she prioritized.

She kept paying minimums on all her debts, but any extra money — even $50 or $100 from a side hustle or a refund — went toward that high-interest card. It became her number one target. She tracked it like a personal challenge. Watching the balance shrink gave her motivation, and every time she made a dent, it felt like winning.

But understanding her debt wasn't just about chasing the biggest number or the scariest interest rate. It was about seeing the full picture—knowing how much was due each month, when payments were scheduled and what options she had.

She started setting calendar reminders for every due date so she would never miss a payment again. She organized her statements in a folder—one tab for each lender—and used a free spreadsheet to track her progress.

One of the most empowering things Sarah did was call each lender. Not to beg or explain, but to ask clear questions:

- What's my current balance?
- What's the interest rate?
- Are there any hardship programs or payment plans?
- Can I set up auto-pay to avoid late fees?

Most of the conversations were straightforward. One lender offered her a lower APR if she set up auto-pay. Another gave her a breakdown of how much of her payment was going to interest vs. principal — and it was eye-opening.

Some people avoid calling their lenders because they're ashamed or afraid of being judged. Sarah had felt that way, too. But what she found was that information is power — and the more she learned, the more confident she became.

Not all debt is created equal. Some, like student loans or mortgages, may be long-term and manageable. Others, like credit card debt, can spiral quickly if left unchecked. The trick is understanding which ones are quietly costing you the most and tackling them strategically.

Sarah's path didn't change overnight. But her mindset did. She went from reacting to her debt to actively managing it. And that shift gave her something she hadn't felt in a long time: momentum.

She created a small ritual every time she made a debt payment — she'd cross out the new balance on her spreadsheet, light a candle, and remind herself, "You're getting closer." It might sound cheesy, but it turned something stressful into something hopeful.

When you understand your debt — when you take the time to lay it all out, sort it, and face it head-on — it stops being a monster in the closet. It becomes a problem with a plan.

And when you have a plan, even a small one, you start to believe that freedom is possible.

For Sarah, understanding her debt wasn't just about numbers. It was about reclaiming her narrative—no longer feeling like a victim of her circumstances but a person with choices, one payment at a time.

Section 5.2: Creating a Debt Payoff Plan

Sarah stared at the whiteboard in her apartment where she had written down all of her debts — neatly listed with balances, due dates and interest rates. It wasn't the prettiest wall art, but it was powerful. For the first time in years, she could see everything clearly.

But seeing it and paying it off were two very different things.

She had made a decision: no more minimum payments just to stay afloat, no more avoiding bills out of fear. She wanted to be *done* with debt—not just survive it. What she needed now was a real plan—one that worked with her lifestyle, gave her momentum and helped her stay consistent.

The question was, where to start?

Sarah began researching debt repayment strategies and quickly came across two common approaches: the **snowball** and the **avalanche**. Both had their merits and both were used by people who had successfully paid off thousands in debt.

The snowball method appealed to her emotionally. It involved paying off the smallest debt first, regardless of the interest rate, then using the payment from that debt to roll into the next smallest — like building a snowball. Sarah loved the idea of quick wins. She imagined knocking out a small $300 credit card balance and feeling that burst of progress.

The avalanche method, on the other hand, targeted the debt with the **highest interest rate** first. It was more mathematically efficient — saving money in the long run by minimizing interest paid.

Sarah's head told her to use the avalanche method. But her heart? It craved the psychological lift of the snowball. She had tried logical approaches before, only to burn out when she didn't feel like she was getting anywhere.

So, she blended the two.

She listed her debts by interest rate but started with one that had a smaller balance and a relatively high APR. It wasn't the absolute worst offender, but it gave her the best of both worlds: a quick win *and* decent interest savings.

Every extra dollar she made — from selling old clothes, babysitting on the weekends, or skipping takeout — went toward that one target debt. She celebrated the day she made the final payment on it like she'd just finished a marathon. It reminded her that progress was possible.

But Sarah also knew she needed consistency, not just bursts of effort. That's when she set up **automated payments**.

At first, she'd been hesitant. She liked the idea of being "in control" each month. But she also knew her schedule — how easy it was to forget a due date or talk herself out of making an extra payment when life got stressful.

So, she automated all her minimum payments to make sure they were never late — and then set up an additional automatic payment, just $50, toward her highest-priority debt. She figured if she made that extra $50 automatic, she wouldn't be tempted to use it elsewhere.

It worked. It became routine. Expected. No more negotiating with herself.

Soon, she increased the extra payment to $75, then $100. When she got a small tax refund, she sent it straight to her next debt. The structure was starting to create momentum.

But not every part of the process was smooth.

One month, her hours were cut at work. Things got tight and she worried she wouldn't be able to keep up. That's when she remembered something a friend had once mentioned: *"You can negotiate with your creditors. They'd rather work with you than risk you defaulting."*

So, she picked up the phone and started making calls. It was uncomfortable at first — that familiar shame crept in — but she pushed through.

To her surprise, most of the reps were understanding. One credit card company offered to lower her APR for six months if she agreed to a fixed payment schedule. Another gave her the option to defer one payment without penalty because she had never missed one before.

It wasn't a magic fix, but it gave her room to breathe.

What stood out most in those calls was this: **creditors are businesses — they want your money, not your silence**. When you communicate with them, especially early, they're often more flexible than you expect.

That experience shifted something in Sarah. She realized that asking for help, or even just for better terms, wasn't weakness — it was strategy.

She kept notes from those calls in a simple notebook, including the names of reps and confirmation numbers. Over time, she built relationships with her lenders, and more importantly, she built confidence in herself.

Month by month, the balances began to shrink. Sarah updated her whiteboard often — crossing off a balance line with a red marker every time she paid off another $500.

She also tracked her "interest saved" total — a number that grew each time she knocked out a high-APR debt. Watching that figure climb reminded her why the hard work mattered.

Yes, there were setbacks. There were months when an unexpected expense — like car repairs or a friend's wedding — slowed her progress. But because she had a clear plan, she always found her way back on track.

She no longer felt like debt was this massive, shapeless monster. It was a series of targets. Some bigger, some smaller. But all of them beatable.

Creating a debt payoff plan wasn't about perfection — it was about **intentionality**.

For Sarah, it started with facing her numbers, choosing a method that worked for her, and committing to action — even when the amounts felt small. The automation kept her consistent, and the negotiation gave her power.

What made the difference wasn't just paying off debt. It was how doing so changed her relationship with money — and with herself.

She went from feeling like debt was something that happened *to* her to something she was taking charge of. And once she had a plan, she knew: this wasn't forever. She had a way out — and she was walking it, one smart step at a time.

Section 5.3: Avoiding Future Debt

The day Sarah made her final credit card payment, she expected to feel relieved — and she did, but the emotion that surprised her most was fear.

She wasn't afraid of debt itself anymore. She'd faced it, worked through it, and climbed out. What she feared now was falling back into it.

She knew how easy it would be to slip — one unexpected bill, one car repair, one impulsive purchase on a bad day. After all, she hadn't racked up her debt on luxury trips or shopping sprees. It had come from little things piling up when she didn't have a cushion.

So, this time, she decided her plan wouldn't stop at being debt-free. Now, she wanted to *stay* free.

The first line of defense was building a safety net — something she'd never really had before: an emergency fund.

For years, the idea of saving three to six months of expenses felt completely out of reach. Back then, she could barely save $20 without needing to use it the following week. But through her debt journey, she'd learned something crucial: starting small was better than not starting at all.

She began by setting a goal of $500. That was enough to cover most car repairs, medical co-pays, or a month of groceries if she lost hours at work. She set up a separate savings account, one she didn't touch except for true emergencies — no "I forgot my sister's birthday" spending allowed.

Each time she got paid; she moved a little into that account. Even $10 here and there added up. Side hustle money? Emergency fund. Tax refund? Emergency fund. Before long, she had $800 saved — more than she'd ever had before in her life.

And that fund changed everything.

The next time her car battery died, she didn't panic or reach for her credit card. She transferred the money, paid the bill, and moved on. It wasn't just about the dollars — it was about the emotional relief. She didn't feel like her financial world was one flat tire away from crumbling.

But Sarah also knew it wasn't just emergencies that could drag her back into debt. She had to change the way she thought about credit itself.

Credit cards had once felt like lifelines — like tools she could use to stretch her income when things got tight. In a way, they were. But they were also traps when used without a plan.

Now that she was out of debt, Sarah didn't cut up all her cards or cancel them in a dramatic gesture. She understood that credit wasn't the enemy — *uncontrolled credit use* was.

So, she kept one card open, mostly for specific purposes like travel or online purchases. But she treated it like a debit card: if she didn't have the money in her account to pay for something immediately, she didn't charge it.

She also set her card to automatically pay in full every month — and kept a low credit limit intentionally, just in case. Her credit score actually improved because of it.

Responsible use, low balances, and on-time payments built her history in a way that protected her, not harmed her.

Still, she kept her eyes open. One of the things debt had taught her was how easily traps can be disguised as opportunities.

She remembered the first time she got a letter saying she'd been "pre-approved" for a higher credit limit. Back then, it felt like a compliment. Now? It felt like a warning.

Debt traps don't always look dangerous at first. They can be shiny offers, like zero-interest financing on a new TV, or "Buy Now, Pay Later" plans that divide payments so small they seem harmless. But Sarah had learned to ask herself a simple question anytime she was tempted: *Would I still buy this if I had to pay for it all today?*

If the answer was no, she passed.

She also stayed alert to emotional spending triggers — especially during stressful times. If she caught herself browsing online stores just to feel better, she'd pause, take a walk, or call a friend. That awareness had become one of her strongest tools.

Of course, Sarah wasn't perfect. No one is. There were months when things were tight, when she had to dip into savings or delay a goal. But the difference now was that she had a plan to *recover*, not spiral.

And she had boundaries.

No co-signing loans for others. No taking on debt for things that weren't essential. No convincing herself that sales were "opportunities" instead of temptations.

Most importantly, she didn't wait until things were falling apart to adjust. If her budget showed signs of strain — like spending more than she'd planned or her emergency fund dipping too low — she course-corrected early. A small change now beat a big crisis later.

As time went on, something shifted in how Sarah thought about debt. It used to be a shadow — always looming behind her. Now, it was just part of her story. A chapter she'd worked through, learned from, and moved beyond.

She didn't fear it anymore because she understood it.

She knew that real financial strength wasn't about never facing debt — it was about building habits, systems, and awareness that made debt unnecessary.

And that's what she carried with her every day: the knowledge that freedom from debt isn't just about paying it off — it's about protecting that freedom once you've earned it.

Chapter 6

Building an Emergency Fund

Section 6.1 – Why an Emergency Fund Matters

The first time Sarah's car broke down, she handled it the way she always had — with her credit card. The repair cost $620, money she didn't have in her bank account. The card was her go-to backup plan, the silent "just in case" she relied on more often than she wanted to admit.

She told herself it wasn't a big deal. She'd pay it off next month. But the next month, something else came up — a doctor's appointment, a forgotten utility bill, then a birthday dinner for her sister. That $620 sat on her card, quietly growing with interest, until it became nearly $900.

That was when Sarah realized she didn't have a debt problem — she had a *safety net* problem.

She wasn't reckless. She wasn't living beyond her means. She just didn't have a buffer. And without that cushion, every bump in the road became a crisis.

That's where the emergency fund comes in. Not as a luxury, not as a someday goal — but as a first line of defense.

Sarah had always thought of an emergency fund as a far-off ideal. "Save three to six months of expenses" sounded overwhelming when she couldn't even get through one month without dipping into overdraft. But once she reframed the way she saw it — not as a mountain to climb, but a tool to *protect* herself — it became something empowering.

The moment she decided to build her emergency fund, something shifted. She wasn't just reacting to money problems anymore — she was preparing for them.

The biggest difference she noticed was emotional.

Before, money stress followed her everywhere. Every unusual sound her car made sent a jolt of panic through her chest. Every unexpected bill felt like it might break her. She kept waiting for something to go wrong — because it always did.

But once she had even a few hundred dollars saved, the fear eased. That little savings account became her shield. Her "breathe easy" money.

The peace of mind it gave her was worth more than the dollars themselves.

She still remembers the first time she had to dip into the fund. Her dog, Max, had gotten sick and needed an emergency vet visit. It cost $400. Instead of reaching for her credit card, she transferred the money from savings.

She didn't have to go into debt. She didn't have to explain to anyone. She just handled it — and refilled the account over the next two paychecks.

That moment was proof: this fund wasn't just about emergencies. It was about freedom.

But building that first layer of savings wasn't easy. Sarah had to fight her old mindset — the voice that said saving only mattered when you had "extra money."

She didn't wait for extra. She *created* it.

She started with a small goal — $500. It was a stretch, but not impossible. She broke it down into $50 increments, and each time she hit a milestone, she celebrated. It didn't matter that it took her a couple of months — what mattered was that she kept going.

The trick wasn't in how much she saved — it was in treating it like a priority. Before, saving had always come last, after bills and groceries and fun. Now, it came first — even if it was just $10 on payday.

She opened a separate savings account at a different bank — one without a debit card or easy access — and nicknamed it "My Peace Fund." The name mattered. It reminded her why it existed: not for shopping, not for vacations, but for the nights when the unexpected showed up and tried to knock her off course.

The beauty of that fund was that it helped prevent future debt.

Sarah had seen it play out again and again in her own life and with friends. Someone would be doing okay financially, but then life would throw a curveball — a job loss, a broken phone, a trip to the ER. Without savings, the credit cards came out. The cycle of debt would begin all over again.

But with an emergency fund, those same curveballs didn't have to derail everything. They were still inconvenient — but not devastating.

And she didn't stop at $500.

Once she reached that first milestone, Sarah set her sights on $1,000. That number gave her even more breathing room — enough to cover the rent if needed, a large medical bill, or a surprise trip out of town to help the family. She wasn't aiming for perfection. She was aiming for *resilience.*

Eventually, she planned to build a fund with three months of expenses — about $6,000 — but she didn't pressure herself to do it all at once. She chipped away at it the same way she had tackled her debt: little by little, with consistency and grace.

One night, while having dinner with a friend who was going through a rough patch, Sarah shared her journey. Her friend had just lost her job and was panicking about how she'd cover rent next month.

Sarah didn't lecture. She didn't hand out unsolicited advice. She just listened — and then gently said, "That's exactly why I started my emergency fund. So, when life throws me something like this, I don't feel like the ground's been pulled out from under me."

Her friend nodded slowly. "I wish I'd started one sooner."

Sarah smiled. "I did too. But the best part is, once you do, everything changes."

That's what building an emergency fund is really about.

It's not about being afraid of emergencies. It's about not letting them control you. It's about creating a little space between *you* and the chaos — so that when life gets unpredictable, you stay grounded.

For Sarah, that fund became more than just money in the bank. It became proof that she could take care of herself. That she was capable of planning ahead. That she didn't have to live in constant reaction mode anymore.

That peace? That calm confidence in the face of uncertainty?

It was worth every dollar.

Section 6.2 – Finding Extra Money to Save

Sarah used to think that saving money required making more money. Every time she heard someone talk about emergency funds or savings goals, she'd get discouraged, assuming it was something that could only happen *after* she got a raise or landed a better job.

But waiting for a bigger paycheck wasn't working. So, she stopped waiting.

She began with one simple goal: find money where it already existed. Not in theory. Not through wishful thinking. But in her actual day-to-day life.

What she learned surprised her.

It started with coffee.

Every morning, Sarah would stop at her favorite café on her way to work. It was a comforting routine — the warm cup in her hands, the quick chat with the barista, the moment of calm before the day began. It cost $5.25. Not a big deal, right?

But one day she did the math: five days a week, four weeks a month — over $100. That was two tanks of gas or a trip to the grocery store.

She didn't quit cold turkey. Instead, she made coffee at home three days a week and still treated herself on Fridays. She saved about $60 a month — and never once felt deprived.

That's when she realized that **saving didn't have to come from sacrifice — just intention**.

She started looking at everything with fresh eyes. The streaming services she didn't really use, the subscription box that was more fun to open than it was actually useful, the groceries that kept going bad in the fridge.

A few tweaks here, a few canceled subscriptions there and suddenly Sarah had carved out almost $200 in monthly breathing room — without earning a dollar more.

That money went straight into her emergency fund.

But Sarah didn't stop at trimming the obvious expenses.

She also got smart about how she handled **unexpected income** — the little windfalls that used to disappear without her even realizing it.

In the past, if she got a tax refund or a small work bonus, it felt like permission to splurge. She'd treat herself, maybe buy new clothes or go out for a fancy dinner. And while that felt good in the moment, it never lasted. By the end of the month, she was back to juggling bills.

This time, she made a new rule: *anything unexpected goes to savings first.*

When she got a $400 refund in the spring, she sent $300 straight into her emergency fund and used the rest for a small night out. When she picked up an extra freelance gig that brought in an unplanned $150, it went right into her "Peace Fund."

These weren't huge sums — but that was the point. Saving wasn't about waiting for big money. It was about treating *all* money as an opportunity.

Sarah also kept a post-it note on her desk that read, "Every extra dollar is a building block." It reminded her that progress didn't have to come in big waves. A trickle was just fine — as long as it kept flowing.

The last shift came when Sarah discovered **automated savings apps**.

She had never been great at remembering to transfer money into savings — especially when life got hectic. She needed something that worked *without* her having to think about it.

That's when a friend introduced her to a round-up app that linked to her debit card and automatically rounded each purchase to the nearest dollar, moving the spare change into a savings account.

At first, it sounded silly — how much could a few cents here and there really add up to? But after the first month, she'd saved nearly $40. Without even noticing.

Then she added a second app that allowed her to schedule small, recurring transfers—$10 every Tuesday. That's it—

no big commitment, no stress, but massive psychological benefit.

Each time she opened the app and saw the balance growing—even slowly—she felt proud—not because she was suddenly rich, but because she was finally consistent.

The apps turned saving from a chore into a background habit. That made all the difference.

Sarah didn't have to change her entire lifestyle to find money for savings. She just had to *pay attention* to how she used what she already had.

By adjusting a few daily habits, being thoughtful about windfalls, and letting technology help her stay on track, she found that saving wasn't out of reach — it had always been possible.

It was never about perfection. Some weeks, she saved only $5; other weeks, she saved $100. But the direction was always forward.

Little by little, her emergency fund grew — not just in dollars, but in meaning.

It became a quiet reminder that she was no longer living at the edge of panic. That she had choices. That she could handle whatever life threw her way — not because she earned six figures, but because she had a plan.

Finding extra money to save wasn't about luck or sacrifice. It was about *intention.* For Sarah, that intention changed everything.

Section 6.3 – Keeping Your Emergency Fund Untouched

When Sarah first started her emergency fund, it felt like a major accomplishment just to get money in the account. Watching the balance grow — \$100, then \$500, then past \$1,000 — gave her a rush of confidence she hadn't felt in years.

But then came the next challenge: *not spending it.*

It's easy to call something an "emergency fund" when it's empty. It's just a good idea, a goal, a concept. But once real money sits in that account, untouched and ready, the temptation to use it starts creeping in.

Sarah felt it the first time she saw a flight deal pop up for a weekend getaway. She'd been working hard, cutting corners, and saving every extra penny. Didn't she *deserve* a break? And hey, the trip was on sale — wasn't that financially smart?

She even hovered over the "purchase" button for a while, telling herself she could replenish the savings after the trip.

But something stopped her.

She thought about how far she'd come. About the car repair she managed to cover last month without using her credit card. About the calm she felt knowing she had a buffer if her job hours were ever cut again.

She realized this wasn't a fund for fun — it was a *lifeline.*

That's when Sarah got serious about protecting her emergency fund from herself.

She moved the money to a high-yield savings account at an online bank — one that wasn't connected to her everyday checking account. It wasn't hard to access, but it wasn't *convenient*, either. There was no debit card. No instant transfer button in her budgeting app.

She called it her "Break Glass" account—a quiet reminder that the money inside was for *emergencies only—not stress-shopping,* flash sales, or last-minute concert tickets.

It didn't mean she couldn't enjoy life. It meant she respected the boundary she'd created for herself.

Still, life happens.

A few months later, Sarah did have to dip into the fund — her dog, Max, needed an unexpected vet procedure, and the bill came to $600. It was exactly what the fund was for. She paid it without hesitation or shame.

But once the crisis passed, she didn't just move on. She made a plan to *rebuild.*

Just like she'd saved in the beginning — small amounts, automatic transfers, and side hustle income — she replenished the $600 over the next two months. Slowly, steadily, without waiting for the "perfect time."

That act of refilling the fund wasn't just about the money. It was about reinforcing the habit. Telling herself: *I use it when I need it — and then I refill it so it's ready again.*

She started treating her emergency fund the way you'd treat the battery in a smoke detector — something you check, maintain, and never let run down without a plan.

But Sarah also knew that temptation would keep showing up.

Sometimes, it looked like boredom — when she wanted to spend just to shake off a bad day. Sometimes, it came disguised as "practicality" — like the time her friend invited her on a last-minute trip and she almost used her emergency savings because it felt like a "rare opportunity."

So, she created a simple mental test before touching the fund. She'd ask herself:

"Is this unexpected?
Is it urgent?
Is it necessary?"

If the answer wasn't yes to all three, she didn't touch the money.

That little pause saved her more than once.

She also built what she called a "buffer fund" — a small, separate savings account for occasional expenses that weren't emergencies but also weren't part of her regular budget. Car maintenance, annual fees, birthdays, and those random things that always pop up.

That buffer fund helped her protect the emergency fund even more. It became her first stop for anything annoying but not critical.

The real lesson Sarah learned was this: having an emergency fund only works if it's *there when you need it.*

It's easy to blur the lines between "emergency" and "inconvenience." But protecting that money means protecting your peace of mind, your financial stability, and the freedom to face life's unexpected turns without falling apart.

Yes, she used it when necessary. But she also honored it. She respected the boundary she'd created.

Every time she resisted dipping into it for something that could wait, she reminded herself of how far she'd come.

This wasn't just about avoiding spending — it was about building discipline and *trusting herself* to make wise choices, even when it wasn't easy.

Years from now, when Sarah looks back at her financial transformation, she won't just remember the moment she paid off a credit card or hit a savings goal.

She'll remember the quiet strength of keeping her emergency fund *untouched* — not because nothing went wrong, but because she had the clarity to know when to use it and the discipline to rebuild it when she did.

That fund was never just cash in a bank. It was a symbol of her growth. And every dollar that stayed safely tucked away was a reminder that she was no longer reacting to life — she was *prepared for it.*

Chapter 7

Improving Your Credit Score

Section 7.1 – Understanding Credit Basics

Sarah had always been nervous around the topic of credit.

She knew it mattered. She'd heard enough stories about friends being denied loans or stuck with sky-high interest rates. But the whole system felt like a mystery — three-digit numbers that seemed to rise and fall for reasons no one could quite explain.

It wasn't until she applied for a rental apartment and got asked about her credit score that reality hit. The landlord mentioned that her score wasn't bad, but it wasn't great either. "You're in the fair range," he said casually, handing back her application. "Not a dealbreaker, but it does raise a few questions."

That phrase — *raises a few questions* — stayed with her.

Sarah realized that her credit score was speaking for her when she wasn't in the room. It was influencing decisions about her housing, job opportunities, car insurance, and even her ability to set up utilities without a deposit. And she'd never really taken the time to understand it.

So, she sat down one weekend and decided to dig in.

What Sarah discovered changed everything.

At its core, a credit score is just a number — usually between 300 and 850 — that tells lenders how likely you are to repay debt. But what makes that number rise or fall isn't random. It's shaped by behaviors. Choices. Patterns.

The score itself is built on several key pieces of information pulled from your credit history. Sarah learned that the biggest factor was her **payment history** — whether she paid her bills on time. Every missed payment could chip away at her score, while a consistent record of on-time payments helped it grow stronger.

Next came **credit utilization** — how much of her available credit she was using. That one surprised her. Sarah had one credit card with a $2,000 limit, and she usually kept a balance of around $1,500 on it. She thought she was doing okay because she was making her minimum payments. But when she ran her numbers, she realized she was using 75% of her available credit — way above the recommended threshold.

She didn't need to pay it all off overnight. But even getting it under 30% — about $600 — could give her score a noticeable boost.

Then came **length of credit history** — how long she'd had credit accounts open. Sarah's student loan, which she'd been paying on for years, actually worked in her favor. The longer a credit account is active and in good standing, the more it helps.

She also found out that **new credit inquiries** played a role. Every time she applied for a new card or loan, her score dipped slightly. It wasn't permanent, but it added up. And **credit mix** — having a variety of credit types like loans and cards — could help, too.

None of these factors were beyond her control.

That's what empowered her most: realizing that her credit score wasn't a verdict — it was a reflection of how she managed her financial relationships.

As Sarah kept reading, she began to see credit not as a threat, but as a tool.

A good score didn't just mean approval for credit cards — it meant *options*. A better rate on a car loan. A stronger rental application. Less stress when dealing with money.

She also began to understand the deeper value of credit health. It wasn't about borrowing more — it was about having *access* if and when she needed it.

Life is unpredictable. If her car broke down tomorrow or she needed to move suddenly, having solid credit would mean she could handle the unexpected without panic.

She remembered the time a few years back when she needed a loan to cover medical costs but got denied because of her thin credit history. At the time, she was embarrassed. Now she saw it clearly: she hadn't done anything wrong — she just hadn't been shown how credit worked.

So, she started small.

She committed to making every payment on time, even if it was just the minimum. She set up automatic payments to make sure she never forgot a due date. She created a plan to bring her card balances down gradually.

She checked her credit reports — free, once a year — and caught a small error on one of them. It was a store card she'd closed but was still showing as active. She disputed it, got it fixed, and saw her score bump up a few points the next month.

It wasn't magic. It was maintenance.

Like brushing her teeth or changing the oil in her car, taking care of her credit became part of her routine. Not dramatic, but steady.

What Sarah learned was that credit isn't just a number — it's a reputation. A quiet record of trust that builds over time.

And like any relationship, it requires care. Pay attention. Show up. Make good on promises.

Improving her credit didn't happen overnight. But by understanding how it worked — and what influenced it — she took back control of something that once felt completely out of her hands.

Credit was no longer a mystery. It was a mirror. Slowly but surely, she was changing the reflection.

Section 7.2 – Fixing Poor Credit

Sarah never forgot the feeling of opening her credit report for the first time.

It was a mix of curiosity and dread — like peeking under the bed to see what monsters were hiding. She had always assumed her credit was "okay," mostly because she didn't want to know if it wasn't. But when she finally sat down, entered her info and pulled her report, she was hit with reality.

Her score was lower than she expected. There were missed payments from two years ago, a medical bill in collections she thought insurance had handled and several maxed-out cards dragging everything down. She felt ashamed. But more than that — she felt stuck.

And that's when she made herself a promise: *I'm not going to hide from this anymore. I'm going to fix it, one step at a time.*

The first thing Sarah noticed as she scrolled through the report was that some of the information didn't look right.

One account showed a missed payment from a date she was sure she had paid on time. Another listed a balance on a card she'd closed out months earlier. At first, she assumed she was misremembering — but then she did something most people don't: she dug deeper.

She logged into her old credit card portal and pulled her transaction history. Sure enough, the payment had been on time. The closed card really did have a $0 balance. And that collection account? It was a duplicate from a billing system error at the hospital.

She learned that credit reports aren't always accurate. In fact, errors are more common than people think. The only way to fix them is to say something.

So, she filed disputes — not with anger, but with clarity. She submitted documentation online to each credit bureau where the errors appeared: Experian, Equifax, and TransUnion. She included screenshots, payment confirmations, and clear explanations.

Within a few weeks, she got updates. Two of the three issues were removed, and her score jumped by almost 30 points.

It wasn't a miracle. It was advocacy. She had learned that when it comes to credit, being quiet doesn't get you anywhere. You have to speak up — because no one else will do it for you.

Next, she turned to the most intimidating part: her balances.

Sarah had three credit cards, all hovering near their limits. The interest alone was costing her hundreds every year. Every month, she made minimum payments and watched almost nothing change.

It felt like trying to empty a bathtub with a spoon.

But instead of letting that frustration paralyze her, Sarah broke the problem down into something manageable. She focused on the card with the smallest balance first — not because it was the cheapest, but because she needed a win.

She scraped together $100 from a side gig, sold a couple of old electronics online, and threw everything extra at that one card. When it hit zero, she felt like she could breathe again.

Then she moved to the next card, and the next. Slowly, her credit utilization dropped from 85% to below 30%. And the more her balances shrank, the more her credit score inched up.

She hadn't changed her income — she'd changed her approach.

She also learned to play defense: she stopped using her cards unless absolutely necessary. She kept one card open with a small recurring subscription on it — just enough to show activity — and set it to auto-pay in full each month. Everything else? On pause.

She wasn't perfect. Sometimes an expense would catch her off guard, and she'd need to use a card. But now, she had a plan for paying it off. She no longer let balances linger for months. She was in control.

A few months in, Sarah heard about something called "authorized users" and wondered if it was just a hack or something that could really work.

After reading more, she realized it could help — if done wisely.

Being added as an authorized user meant someone else — usually a family member or partner — added her to their credit card account. She wouldn't be responsible for the payments, and the account's history would show up on her credit report.

The key was choosing someone who had strong credit habits: a low balance, a long account history, and no late payments.

She talked to her older sister, who had excellent credit and had always managed her finances well. At first, Sarah was nervous to ask — it felt like admitting failure. But her sister understood. She added Sarah to her card as an authorized user without giving her a physical card to spend with.

Within a month, the history of that account showed up on Sarah's credit report — and her score rose again.

This wasn't a shortcut or a cheat. It was a smart strategy. A way to show lenders that she could be associated with a positive credit history.

It didn't erase her past — but it helped balance it.

The journey to repair her credit wasn't quick. But Sarah's relationship with money — and with herself — changed in the process.

She no longer saw her score as a permanent judgment. It was simply feedback, and feedback could be improved.

By facing the errors, paying down her balances with intention, and wisely using tools like authorized user status, she turned her credit story around — one choice at a time.

Fixing poor credit isn't about shame. It's about rebuilding trust — with lenders, yes, but more importantly, with yourself.

Once Sarah realized that she didn't just raise her score. She raised her standards.

Section 7.3 – Maintaining Good Credit

After months of hard work, Sarah had finally pulled her credit score into the "good" range. She wasn't where she ultimately wanted to be just yet, but the progress she'd made was real — and hard-earned.

Still, as proud as she was, a quiet thought kept tapping on her shoulder: *What if I mess it up again?*

It wasn't that she didn't trust herself. It's just that for a long time, credit had felt like something that happened *to* her, not something she actively managed. Now that she had taken control, she didn't want to let go of the progress she'd fought so hard to achieve.

Sarah knew she needed a plan — not just for fixing her credit, but for *protecting* it.

The first shift she made was in how she used credit day-to-day.

Before, credit cards had been her safety net. If something unexpected popped up — dinner out, car trouble, new clothes — she'd swipe first and worry later.

Now, credit wasn't her emergency plan. It was a tool she used carefully, like a sharp knife in the kitchen: incredibly helpful, but dangerous if handled carelessly.

Sarah decided to use her credit card for only one recurring expense each month — her Spotify subscription. It was small, predictable, and easy to pay off. That simple move ensured her card stayed active and continued building a positive payment history, while never putting her at risk of racking up a balance.

She set up automatic payments for that card to pay in full each month. That way, she never missed a due date, never paid interest and never had to remember to log in and do it manually.

More than anything, she respected the card. She no longer viewed it as "extra money," and she made peace with the fact that not everything needed to go on credit. If she couldn't afford something in cash, she waited.

It was a quiet kind of discipline — but it made all the difference.

Another change was how she thought about her credit utilization.

In the past, Sarah hadn't even known what that meant. She'd assumed that as long as she didn't max out her cards, she was doing fine. But through her journey, she'd learned that keeping her balances *low* — ideally under 30% of her available credit — was key to keeping her score healthy.

Even better, under 10% was where the real credit score improvements happened.

So even when she used her card responsibly, she watched that number closely. If her limit was $2,000, she never let her balance go above $600 — and she made early payments if she got close.

Some months were tighter than others. Sometimes a surprise expense pushed her closer to that limit than she liked. But now she knew how to recover: make a partial payment mid-cycle, bring the balance down quickly, and communicate with her bank if needed.

Managing credit was no longer about avoiding mistakes. It was about *responding* wisely when things didn't go perfectly.

The final habit Sarah built was one of the most important — and the easiest to overlook: regularly checking her credit reports.

Before, she had been afraid to look. Now, she understood that knowledge was power. Mistakes happened and catching them early could make or break her score.

She signed up for a free credit monitoring tool, one that alerted her anytime a new account appeared on her report or a change in her score occurred. She also marked her calendar to pull her full credit reports — from all three bureaus — every four months, cycling through them so she could check one at a time throughout the year.

It became part of her self-care routine. Just like checking in on her budget or reviewing her savings goals, monitoring her credit reminded her that she was *actively* in charge of her financial well-being.

Once, she noticed a small collection account pop up that didn't look familiar. She caught it early — within weeks of it being reported — and was able to call the agency and resolve it before it did lasting damage. It turned out to be a billing error from an old internet provider. The old version of Sarah might have ignored it out of fear or frustration. The new version made one phone call and kept her score safe.

Maintaining good credit wasn't dramatic. It wasn't about huge swings or sudden boosts. It was about *consistency* — showing up, paying attention and making small, steady choices that added up over time.

Sarah didn't need to obsess over every point on her score. She just needed to protect the habits that got her here: using credit carefully, keeping balances low, and staying informed.

Most importantly, she gave herself grace. Credit wasn't a moral judgment — it was a system. One she had learned to work with, not against.

Now, her credit wasn't a source of anxiety. It was a quiet foundation beneath her — supporting her decisions, backing her up when life got messy, and opening doors she never thought she could walk through.

Good credit, she realized, didn't change who you are. But it *amplifies* your ability to move forward. That made every responsible choice — no matter how small — completely worth it.

Chapter 8

Saving for the Future (Even When You're Broke)

Section 8.1 – Automating Savings

When Sarah first heard the phrase "pay yourself first," she almost laughed out loud. At the time, she was barely making it from paycheck to paycheck. There was no "extra" money to save, no cushion to speak of. Every dollar she earned had somewhere it needed to go: bills, groceries, gas and the occasional coffee to keep her sane.

Still, she couldn't shake the idea.

What if saving wasn't about *having* extra — but about *prioritizing* herself, even when things were tight? What if, instead of waiting for the perfect moment to start saving, she just started now, with whatever she could?

That tiny mental shift changed everything.

It began with $5.

Sarah logged into her online banking and set up an automatic transfer from her checking account to her savings account every payday — $5, scheduled to move the morning after her direct deposit hit.

It was so small that she barely noticed it was gone, but every time she checked her account and saw the growing total — even if it was just $20, then $40 — she felt something powerful: progress.

That's when she realized the beauty of automation.

She didn't have to *decide* to save money each week. She didn't have to fight herself or wait until the end of the month to see what was left over. The decision had already been made. That one decision — made once — kept paying off again and again.

Soon, she bumped the transfer to $10, then $15. Whenever she got a raise or found a little extra from a side gig, she adjusted the amount. She made the transfer happen on the same day as payday so she wouldn't be tempted to spend it.

The key wasn't the amount — it was the consistency.

Sarah started calling it "stealth saving." It happened quietly in the background, without any fanfare, until one day, she looked up and realized she'd saved more than $500 without feeling like she had "sacrificed" a thing.

Then, she discovered a round-up savings app.

At first, she was skeptical. Could spare change really make a difference? But she decided to try it. She linked her debit card to the app, and every time she made a purchase, it rounded the amount up to the nearest dollar and transferred the difference into savings.

$4.50 for coffee? $0.50 to savings.
$19.70 at the grocery store? $0.30 to savings.

It was effortless. And oddly satisfying.

After a few weeks, she checked the app and saw she'd saved nearly $40 — money she hadn't even noticed missing. That $40 became the beginning of her travel fund.

What made these tools so helpful wasn't that they did the saving for her — it was that they *removed the friction*.

No more waiting until the end of the month to see what was left. No more trying to manually move money around (and then changing her mind when things got tight). No more guilt. Just quiet, consistent progress.

But perhaps the most powerful thing Sarah did was fully embrace the "pay yourself first" mindset.

For most of her life, she had saved reactively — if there was money left after rent, bills, and everything else, she might tuck some away. But there was never money left.

When she flipped the script and began treating saving like a *bill* — something due to herself, not optional — she felt more in control.

It didn't mean she saved hundreds of dollars a month—sometimes it was $25, sometimes just $10—but it was *intentional.*

She wasn't waiting for permission anymore.

Because it was automatic, she didn't have to think about it every day. The effort happened once — the benefits compounded over time.

Of course, there were weeks when things were tight, times when she had to pause or adjust her savings and that was okay.

The point wasn't perfection. It was *habit.*

Even when she had to skip a transfer, she didn't beat herself up. She just picked it back up the next week. She'd come too far to let one bump in the road knock her off course.

Now, when she looked at her savings account, she didn't just see numbers — she saw stability. Possibility. Proof that even when you feel broke, you can still build a future.

Automating her savings helped Sarah overcome the biggest hurdle most people face: starting. It made saving feel *doable*, even in small doses.

She didn't have to be rich. She just had to be consistent.

That consistency—born out of a simple $5 transfer—became the foundation of her financial security.

Saving for the future, she realized, isn't about how much you make. It's about making a habit of choosing yourself. Automate that choice, and everything else gets easier.

Section 8.2 – Investing Small Amounts

When Sarah used to think about investing, the image in her mind looked nothing like her life. She pictured suits, stock tickers, and people with six-figure incomes making bold financial moves. It felt out of reach — a language she hadn't been taught, a club she didn't belong to.

For years, she avoided the topic entirely. It was easier to focus on paying off debt, building an emergency fund, and surviving the month. But something shifted the day she read an article that said: *"You don't need to be wealthy to start investing — you build wealth by starting where you are."*

That line stuck with her.

So, she started looking into ways to invest without needing thousands of dollars — and what she found surprised her. Investing wasn't just for people with Wall Street connections or massive salaries. There were platforms designed for beginners, for people like her, with just a few dollars to spare.

Sarah started with **micro-investing**.

She downloaded an app that let her start with just $5. It is linked to her checking account, and, similar to her round-up savings app, it invests in her spare change from everyday purchases. Every coffee, every lunch, every random drugstore run — a few cents here and there were quietly redirected into an investment portfolio.

At first, she didn't think it would amount to much. But over time, those cents turned into dollars. And those dollars, thanks to market growth and reinvested earnings, started to grow even more.

It wasn't about becoming rich overnight — it was about building muscle.

Sarah began checking her app once a week, not to obsess over gains or losses but to reinforce the habit. Seeing her balance inch upward, knowing it was money she wasn't even missing day-to-day, gave her a sense of quiet momentum.

She'd always believed investing was risky — and yes, markets do go up and down — but what she realized was that *not* investing carried its own risk: the risk of missing out on long-term growth.

That's when she became curious about reinvestment.

One evening, Sarah stumbled upon a term she hadn't heard before: **Dividend Reinvestment Plans**, or DRIPs.

She learned that some companies pay out dividends — small payments made to shareholders, usually quarterly. But instead of pocketing those dividends as cash, DRIPs automatically reinvest them into buying more shares of that company. No action needed. No fees.

It sounded small. But Sarah had learned that *small* is where everything starts.

She opened a brokerage account and bought a couple of fractional shares of companies she used every day — brands she trusted. When dividends were paid, they didn't land in her bank account. They went straight back into buying more stock.

It was slow, steady growth. But that's what made it sustainable.

DRIPs reminded Sarah a lot of her automated savings — make the decision once and let the system do the rest. She didn't need to track payouts or time the market. Her role was simple: contribute what she could and stay consistent.

Still, there were days when the market dipped, and she'd feel a jolt of anxiety. Had she made a mistake? Was she wasting money by investing instead of saving?

That's when she learned about **dollar-cost averaging** — a strategy that gave her peace of mind.

Rather than trying to guess when the best time to invest was — something even professional investors struggle with —

she committed to investing the same amount of money on a regular schedule. For Sarah, that meant $25 every month, rain or shine.

Some months, that $25 would buy more shares if prices were low. Other months, it would buy fewer. But over time, it would average out. More importantly, it kept her from panicking during market drops or getting too overconfident during booms.

Dollar-cost averaging gave her emotional distance — and in investing, that's invaluable.

She treated it like brushing her teeth: something routine, simple, and necessary for long-term health. Not exciting, maybe. But effective.

Sarah wasn't trying to become a day trader. She didn't spend hours reading financial reports or watching the news for market trends. What she cared about was building a future — slowly, responsibly, and on her terms.

She set reminders every quarter to review her investments. If she had a little extra that month, she'd toss it into her account. If things were tight, she stuck with the minimum. The point wasn't perfection. The point was *showing up.*

She also stopped comparing herself to people who were further along—the friend who maxed out her 401(k) and the coworker who talked about "diversifying" his portfolio like it was second nature.

Sarah reminded herself that she was still early in the game — and the earlier she started, even with small amounts, the more time her money had to grow.

She learned to celebrate the quiet milestones: her first $500 invested. Her first dividend was reinvested. The first time, her balance grew by more than she'd contributed that month.

These weren't financial fireworks — but they were proof. Proof that she was building something real.

Investing small amounts didn't transform Sarah's life overnight. But it *changed her identity*.

She no longer saw herself as someone who couldn't afford to invest. She was an investor. She was participating. She was planting seeds.

As those seeds slowly grew, so did her confidence.

She didn't need to be wealthy to invest — she needed to be consistent.

By starting where she was, with what she had, Sarah was shaping a future she once thought belonged only to other people.

Turns out, it belonged to her too.

Section 8.3 – Long-Term Financial Planning

For a long time, Sarah avoided thinking too far ahead.

Retirement? That felt like another lifetime. A distant fantasy reserved for people who wore business suits, had financial advisors, or made more in a month than she made in a year. Planning for "the future" just didn't feel like it applied to someone still figuring out how to make rent on time.

But life has a funny way of forcing perspective.

One evening, she sat with her mom, helping her sort through paperwork after a recent surgery. As they reviewed medical bills, Social Security forms, and a modest pension plan, Sarah saw the stress in her mother's eyes—not just about her health but also about money.

That's when it hit her.

One day, I'll be the age my mom is now. And what I do today will decide what that version of me lives with — or lives without.

That night, Sarah decided it was time to stop thinking of long-term financial planning as something "for rich people." It was for her, too — maybe even more so.

She started small, as she always did.

The first time she heard about a 401(k), it sounded confusing — acronyms, contribution limits, vesting schedules. But when she broke it down, she saw the simplicity hiding beneath the jargon: this was a way to let her future self get paid.

Her job didn't offer a 401(k), so she opened a **Roth IRA** instead—a retirement account she could contribute to independently. What made it feel manageable was knowing she didn't need to max it out right away—she just needed to begin.

She set up $25 automatic transfers each month. It didn't feel like much, but she reminded herself: *compound interest isn't about size — it's about time.* Starting now, even with tiny amounts, was worth far more than waiting until she felt "ready."

As her income grew and her financial habits got stronger, she upped her contribution little by little. There were months when she skipped it. Life happened. But the key was returning to it, again and again.

What she loved about her Roth IRA was how it gave her a sense of ownership over her future. The money didn't disappear into a black hole — she could log in and watch it grow, even if slowly. It was hers. A nest egg. A lifeboat. A promise.

And over time, that promise started to shape her goals.

Sarah stumbled onto the concept of **financial independence** one night while scrolling through personal finance blogs.

It wasn't about getting rich. It was about freedom — the idea that with enough intention and preparation, you could create a life where money didn't dictate every decision. A life where you worked because you wanted to, not because you *had* to.

The phrase that stuck with her was: *money buys choices.*

She didn't need millions to feel secure. But she wanted the ability to walk away from a toxic job. To take time off if a family member needed her. To retire on her own terms — not work until exhaustion forced her hand.

So, she started defining her version of freedom.

For her, it wasn't a beach house or early retirement at 40. It was stability—room to breathe. Maybe buying a home one day. Maybe traveling without guilt. Maybe just knowing that if she lost her job, she wouldn't be drowning in panic.

Those goals gave her fuel. They helped her look past the short-term discomfort of saving and focus on the long-term life she wanted to build.

She built a vision board — not with luxury cars or mansions, but with images that represented peace: a cozy home, a passport, a hiking trail. Every time she made a financial decision, she asked: *Does this bring me closer to that life?*

Sometimes, it meant saying no to things in the moment. But saying no now meant saying yes later — to freedom, to choices, to security.

As she started looking further ahead, Sarah realized long-term planning wasn't just about retirement. It was about **life events** — the predictable ones and the unexpected ones.

She thought about getting married one day. Maybe having a child. Maybe taking a year off to care for a parent or go back to school. She knew these things weren't guaranteed, but they were possibilities — and she wanted to meet them prepared, not panicked.

So, she started naming them—not all at once, not with pressure—just enough to acknowledge their place in her life. She created little "future funds" for different dreams and milestones.

A few dollars here and there went into a savings account labeled "Big Life Moves." She didn't know exactly what it would be used for yet — but that was the point. When something big came along, she'd have a head start.

Planning for the future didn't mean predicting it perfectly. It meant building a foundation so that whatever came, she could meet it standing tall.

Sarah often thought back to that moment with her mom — the fear in her eyes as she wondered if she'd have enough to cover her needs. That memory stayed with her, not as something to fear but as something to prepare for.

And with every contribution to her retirement account, every goal set, every decision made with tomorrow in mind,

Sarah built not just a savings plan — but a safety net for the woman she'd one day become.

She learned that long-term financial planning isn't reserved for the wealthy. It's an act of love. A way of saying to your future self, *I see you. I've got you.*

That kind of security? It's worth building, one small step at a time.

Chapter 9

Mindset and Emotional Control Around Money

Section 9.1 – Overcoming Financial Anxiety

For years, Sarah's relationship with money could be summed up in one word: *fear.*

Every time she opened her banking app, a wave of anxiety rushed over her. Her stomach would twist, her shoulders would tense, and her mind would spiral into "what ifs." What if her rent check bounced? What if she forgot about a bill? What if she couldn't afford something unexpected?

Even when things were okay — when she had just enough to cover her needs — the fear didn't go away. It lived in the background like static, always buzzing, always draining.

It took Sarah a long time to realize that her anxiety wasn't just about money itself. It was about *how she thought about money.* The stories she told herself. The beliefs she carried.

The way her brain had been trained to panic before she even did the math.

One night, after a particularly stressful week, Sarah sat down with a notebook and wrote out every thought that came to her mind when she thought about her finances.

I'll never get ahead.
I'm not good with money.
Something bad is always about to happen.
I should have figured this out by now.

Looking at that list felt like holding up a mirror to her own self-doubt. But it also sparked a realization: *These thoughts aren't facts. They're patterns. And I have the power to change them.*

She started practicing awareness. The next time she caught herself thinking, "I'll never get ahead," she paused and asked, "Is that really true?"

The truth was, she *had* gotten ahead in small ways. She'd paid off a credit card. Built an emergency fund. Started saving for the future. No, she wasn't where she wanted to be yet — but she was moving. And that mattered.

This was the beginning of Sarah's mindset shift.

Reframing how she talked to herself about money didn't happen overnight. It wasn't some magical affirmation that fixed everything. It was small, daily decisions to speak to herself with more grace.

When she made a mistake — like overspending or forgetting a bill — instead of spiraling into shame, she said, *"Okay. That happened. What can I learn? What can I do next?"*

She replaced harsh internal monologues with questions:
Instead of "Why am I so behind?"
She asked, "What's one small thing I can do today to feel more in control?"

This wasn't about being delusional or pretending everything was perfect. It was about breaking the cycle of hopelessness — the belief that because money had once been a source of stress, it always would be.

She also started focusing on *what she could control.* Not the past, not the system, not the bills she didn't expect. But her reactions. Her next step. Her mindset.

That shift created space — space to breathe, to forgive herself, to believe that she wasn't broken just because her finances weren't perfect.

But one of the most powerful tools Sarah found in overcoming financial anxiety was gratitude.

It wasn't always easy to feel thankful when money was tight. Some days, it felt like the last thing she wanted to do. But even on her hardest days, she started listing three things she was grateful for — and often, they were things money had touched:

- A fridge with groceries
- The bus pass that got her to work
- The cozy sweater she found on sale that made her feel confident

Gratitude didn't erase her anxiety, but it softened it.

It reminded her of what *was* working. It grounded her in the present. It helped her see that even though her financial situation wasn't where she wanted it to be, it wasn't without blessings.

Over time, those moments of gratitude added up. They shifted the emotional weight she carried around money. Instead of constantly focusing on scarcity, she began noticing sufficiency — not abundance in the flashy sense, but enoughness.

Enough to take the next step.
Enough to rest without guilt.
Enough to feel hopeful again.

One afternoon, while helping a friend set up a simple budget, Sarah realized how far she'd come.

Her friend was frustrated, overwhelmed, and ashamed of how often she avoided her bank account. And Sarah recognized that feeling like it had been yesterday.

She didn't offer a spreadsheet or a lecture. Instead, she said, "I used to feel the exact same way. But things started to change when I stopped treating money like a monster and started treating it like a relationship."

Her friend looked confused, so Sarah continued: "You don't fix a relationship by ignoring it or yelling at it. You fix it by showing up. Even when it's awkward. Even when you're scared. Especially when you're scared."

Overcoming financial anxiety isn't about reaching a certain dollar amount. It's about healing the way you *think* about money.

It's about recognizing when your thoughts are rooted in fear, choosing to reframe those thoughts with compassion, and reminding yourself of what's already working — even when it feels small.

Sarah still has moments of doubt. We all do. But now, she meets those moments with curiosity instead of criticism.

She doesn't run from her bank account anymore. She opens it with purpose, knowing that whatever it says, she has the power to move forward.

Because peace around money doesn't come from perfection — it comes from perspective.

That perspective is something you build, one gentle thought at a time.

Section 9.2 – Developing a Healthy Relationship with Money

For most of her adult life, Sarah had connected her financial situation to her self-worth.

If her bank account was low, she felt low. When she got an overdraft notice, she felt like a failure. If someone else seemed to be "doing better" financially — buying a new car, going on vacation, posting yet another polished milestone online — she'd shrink inside, wondering what was wrong with her.

She wouldn't have admitted it out loud, but deep down, Sarah believed that how much she had — or didn't have — was a reflection of who she was.

It wasn't until a conversation with a friend opened her eyes.

They were sitting in a coffee shop, catching up on life. Sarah mentioned how embarrassed she'd felt buying groceries the week before when her card declined because she forgot a transfer hadn't gone through. She'd laughed it off in the moment, but the shame had stuck with her all week.

Her friend didn't flinch. "That's happened to me, too," she said. "And it sucked. But it doesn't mean you're less than. It just means you're human."

Sarah blinked. That sentence, so simple and so kind, planted a seed.

From that moment forward, she began to question the invisible links she'd created between money and identity.

Where had she learned that being "good with money" meant you were better, smarter, more worthy? That having financial struggles meant you were irresponsible or broken?

She started to unpack the messages — from childhood, from media, from the culture around her — that told her wealth equaled success, and struggle meant shame.

Little by little, she began to separate who she *was* from what she *had*.

This wasn't denial. She still believed in financial growth and responsibility. But she also believed in self-compassion. She could make mistakes without making them mean everything.

Sarah began treating her relationship with money the way you might treat a relationship with a close friend: with honesty, consistency, and kindness.

To help shift her mindset, Sarah started using simple affirmations. Not the kind that felt forced or fluffy, but grounded, intentional reminders to reset her inner dialogue.

She wrote them on sticky notes and placed them around her apartment — by her mirror, on her fridge, near her laptop:

- "I am learning how to take care of my money."
- "My value is not measured by my income."
- "I make progress every day, even in small steps."

At first, it felt awkward. Like she was pretending. But with repetition, something changed. The affirmations didn't erase her challenges — they rewired the way she approached them.

They softened the shame.
They gave her language for grace.

They reminded her that building a better relationship with money was just that — a *relationship*, not a race.

Over time, these words turned into habits. She stopped criticizing herself for small setbacks. She celebrated tiny wins. She tracked her progress with curiosity instead of judgment.

The hardest part, though, was letting go of comparison.

Sarah didn't consider herself envious, but social media had a way of making her feel like everyone else was miles ahead. Engagement announcements came with diamond rings. Housewarming parties were for homes she couldn't dream of affording. Even "humble" vacation posts made her feel like she was behind.

One day, while scrolling through photos of a friend's new condo, she felt a familiar ache. *Why not me?*

But this time, instead of spiraling, she closed the app and whispered out loud, "Their timeline isn't mine."

She repeated that line often. Because it was true.

Everyone's financial journey is different. Some people start with support, others work three jobs just to break even, some make mistakes and recover quickly and others carry invisible burdens that make even small wins feel monumental.

Sarah began to focus on her own lane. She measured progress against *where she'd been*, not against someone else's highlight reel.

When comparison popped up, she treated it like a signal — a reminder to ground herself in gratitude and redirect her energy toward her goals.

She built a vision for her life based on what mattered to *her*—not what looked impressive or got likes, but what made her feel free, peaceful, and proud.

In time, Sarah's relationship with money began to mirror her relationship with herself — a work in progress, full of ups and downs, but rooted in growth.

She no longer viewed her finances as a report card. She viewed them as a conversation. A process. A partnership.

She didn't need to be rich to feel empowered. She just needed to feel connected — to her values, her efforts, and her worth.

That worth? It was never tied to a number.

It lived in how she showed up. In how she kept going. In how she treated herself through every rise and fall.

Because a healthy relationship with money doesn't start in your bank account. It starts in your mind — and in the quiet, compassionate belief that you are enough, no matter what.

Section 9.3 – Staying Motivated Through Setbacks

Sarah had just hit a milestone — her emergency fund had reached $1,000, her credit score had improved, and she was starting to feel like she was finally gaining traction.

Then her car broke down.

The repair bill was nearly $900, and just like that, most of her emergency savings were gone. She sat in her car afterward, hands gripping the steering wheel, angry and exhausted. It wasn't fair. She'd been doing everything right — budgeting, saving, staying disciplined — and it still felt like she was treading water.

In that moment, she considered giving up. Not on life, but on the effort. On all the careful planning and small wins that suddenly seemed pointless.

But after the tears dried and the frustration settled, something deeper took hold. A quiet reminder: *This is why I started saving in the first place.*

Setbacks weren't proof of failure. They were proof of *life.* Unpredictable, inconvenient, sometimes expensive — but normal.

How she chose to respond would define her financial journey far more than any single moment of progress ever could.

Sarah started to look at that repair — and other setbacks that followed — differently. Not as roadblocks but as checkpoints. Points where she could pause, reassess and *learn.*

Before, a setback like that would have sent her spiraling into debt or emotional spending. But this time, she covered the cost with money she had *intentionally* saved. That mattered. Even though her balance dropped, her self-trust didn't.

What surprised her most was how freeing that mindset was. Instead of obsessing over what she'd "lost," she focused on what she'd gained: resilience.

She gave herself permission to slow down — and even to readjust her goals.

Originally, she had planned to have $3,000 saved by the end of the year. But after covering the repair, she adjusted that to $2,000. At first, she felt like she was letting herself down. But then she remembered: *Life changes and your goals are allowed to change with it.*

Flexibility wasn't failure. It was *wisdom.*

She rewrote her savings plan, added a few extra months to her timeline, and removed the pressure to "make up" for lost ground. In doing so, she created space to breathe.

Because goals should be motivating — not punishing.

There were other setbacks, too—months when work was slow, unexpected bills, times when she slipped back into old habits—overspending on takeout or skipping her budget check-ins. But what changed everything was how she responded to those moments.

She stopped treating setbacks as reasons to start over and saw them as part of the process—a necessary part.

Each one offered a chance to ask, *What went wrong? What can I do differently next time? What's the next best step from here?*

Instead of spiraling into shame, she shifted into reflection.

It wasn't always easy. There were days when she felt discouraged like nothing she did would ever be enough. But over time, she built something stronger than motivation: *resilience.*

Motivation comes and goes. It's fueled by good days and progress. But resilience? That's what carries you through the hard days. The flat months. The moments where the path ahead feels blurry.

Sarah learned to celebrate consistency more than perfection. Even when she had to pause contributions, she stayed connected to her goals. She reminded herself that falling down didn't mean falling apart.

It meant she was human — and healing her relationship with money in real time.

One of her favorite things to do, especially after a tough financial hit, was revisit her journal. Not the numbers — but the *feelings.* She'd read back on old entries, where she once felt overwhelmed, and realize just how far she'd come.

Even with setbacks, she was making progress. Not just in her account balance, but in her mindset, her behavior, and her self-trust.

Each hurdle became another layer of strength.

She started collecting quotes that reminded her of her why. She stuck them to her bathroom mirror, kept them in her phone notes. One of her favorites was: *"Progress is not linear — but it's still progress."*

And when her inner critic got loud — when that voice said, "You're behind. You messed up. You're not doing enough." — she met it with something stronger: grace.

Grace told her that progress was messy. That the work still counted. That rebuilding wasn't starting over — it was starting *stronger.*

Sarah learned that staying motivated through setbacks wasn't about being endlessly optimistic. It was about being *realistic* and *resilient.* It was about showing up — again and again — even when the numbers didn't look the way she wanted them to. Even when life got in the way.

Every time she bounced back, her confidence grew.

She trusted herself a little more. Believed a little deeper in her ability to reach the future she was working for.

Because setbacks will happen. But giving up doesn't have to.

Sometimes, the most powerful financial choice you can make is simply deciding: *I'm not quitting. I'm adjusting — and I'm continuing forward.*

Chapter 10

Creating a Sustainable Financial Plan

Section 10.1 – Reviewing and Adjusting the Budget

At the beginning of her budgeting journey, Sarah treated her budget like a sacred contract. Once she wrote it down — rent, groceries, transportation, savings — she expected to follow it perfectly.

But by the third week of the month, reality would set in.

She'd underestimated how much she'd spend on groceries. A surprise birthday dinner for a friend hadn't been in the plan. Gas prices spiked. And suddenly, the neat little plan she had created at the start of the month felt like a lie.

At first, she saw this as failure. She'd beat herself up for "not sticking to the budget" and often abandoned the plan altogether by the time the month ended.

It wasn't until she shifted her mindset that things started to click. A budget wasn't supposed to be rigid — it was supposed to be responsive.

Sarah began to think of her budget like a living document — one that moved and changed with her life. Instead of writing it once and hoping for the best, she made reviewing her budget a regular practice.

Every Sunday evening, she'd carve out 20 minutes to sit with her numbers. She'd pull up her bank app, open her spreadsheet or notebook, and go line by line through her week. Not with judgment — but with curiosity.

Where did her money actually go?
What categories were working?
Where was she over?
What surprised her?

This small ritual helped her stay connected to her spending in real time, not just at the end of the month when it was too late to adjust. And more importantly, it helped her get *better* at budgeting — not through strict discipline, but through observation.

Over time, Sarah noticed patterns. She consistently overestimated her willpower around takeout — it was a comfort at the end of long workdays. Instead of trying to eliminate that habit, she made room for it in the budget. She increased her "dining out" line and reduced her streaming subscriptions instead.

That one change didn't just improve her numbers — it improved her *relationship* with the budget. She wasn't trying to force herself into someone else's version of "financial discipline." She was building a system that actually fit her life.

Another month, Sarah realized she had budgeted $100 for clothing but hadn't bought anything at all. Meanwhile, she'd had to dip into her emergency fund to pay for car maintenance she hadn't anticipated.

That's when she learned to be more flexible with her categories.

She moved the unused clothing money into a "car fund" for next time. Then, she created a few flexible buckets in her budget labeled "seasonal expenses" and "just in case." These weren't rigid categories with fixed spending expectations — they were buffers for the unexpected.

Suddenly, those unexpected expenses felt less like surprises and more like part of the plan.

Sarah also realized that budgets don't just teach you about numbers — they teach you about *yourself.*

One month, she noticed she had overspent on entertainment three weeks in a row. Instead of scolding herself, she dug deeper: What was she avoiding? What was she trying to feel better about?

She realized she'd been lonely. Her job had been isolating lately, and streaming movies and ordering comfort food had become a coping mechanism. That insight didn't just help her budget — it helped her prioritize connection.

She scheduled a few free hangouts with friends instead of defaulting to takeout. She felt better — and spent less — not by cutting, but by understanding.

Perhaps the most powerful shift Sarah made was in how she responded to mistakes.

Before, going over budget felt like proof she couldn't be trusted with money. Now, it felt like feedback.

Every mistake carried a lesson — and often, those lessons led to smarter choices.

She didn't try to get every category right on the first try. She allowed herself room to adjust. Some months, she spent more on groceries because she had family visiting. Other months, she saved extra because her spending was naturally lower.

The difference now was that she stayed *engaged.* She kept coming back to the process.

She stopped looking for a perfect budget and started building a *realistic* one — a plan that could stretch when life required it, but always pulled her back on course.

Sarah's monthly review became one of her most empowering habits.

It wasn't flashy. It didn't come with gold stars or instant gratification. But it grounded her. It reminded her of where her money was going, what it was doing for her, and how to keep refining the plan as life unfolded.

Budgeting wasn't a one-time act of willpower. It was an ongoing conversation — one where she got to ask questions, make edits, and grow into the kind of financial life she wanted.

By treating her budget like a tool — not a test — Sarah built something far more valuable than a spreadsheet. She built trust in herself. The kind that doesn't disappear when plans change, or mistakes happen.

Because in the end, reviewing and adjusting her budget wasn't about control. It was about *connection.* And with that connection came confidence — the kind that lasts, no matter what the month throws her way.

Section 10.2 – Preparing for Future Financial Goals

Sarah was sitting at her kitchen table one Saturday morning, sipping coffee and flipping through a notebook where she had been tracking her spending and savings for the last year. There was a sense of pride in how far she had come — the debt she'd paid down, the emergency fund she'd built, the budget she'd finally made work for her life.

But now, as she looked ahead, a different question began to form: *What am I building this for?*

Saving just to save had helped her develop discipline. But saving with purpose — that was a whole different level of motivation.

That's when Sarah realized it was time to shift her thinking from stability to strategy. She wasn't just trying to stay afloat anymore. She was ready to swim toward something bigger.

The first goal she wrote down was small but meaningful: a weekend getaway with her sister. They hadn't taken a trip together in years, and she wanted it to be paid for in cash. That meant setting aside around $400 over the next four months.

It felt doable. Clear. Exciting.

But alongside that short-term plan, Sarah started thinking about the long game. What did she want life to look like five years from now? Ten? Was she hoping to buy a home? Go back to school? Launch her own business?

She didn't have all the answers, but she started writing out ideas.

A "house savings fund."
A "career pivot" account.
A reminder to increase her retirement contributions next year.

These weren't just items on a list — they were *intentions.* And naming them gave her a sense of direction she hadn't felt before.

From there, she began setting new savings and investment targets — not because someone told her what she "should" save, but because she was creating a financial life that fit her actual dreams.

It wasn't about hitting every number perfectly. It was about moving with purpose.

Of course, with goals came decisions. And planning for major expenses meant looking at the road ahead with honesty.

Sarah knew her car wouldn't last forever. The check engine light had been flickering on and off, and while it still ran fine most days, she didn't want to wait until it broke down to start preparing.

So, she opened a separate savings account and named it "Next Car." No pressure. No rush. Just a space to slowly build what she'd need.

At the same time, she started thinking about healthcare costs, travel, and even weddings — not just her own, if she ever got married, but the costs of attending friends' ceremonies, buying gifts, and traveling for events.

By identifying these major life expenses before they hit, Sarah gave herself the gift of time. She could save gradually, in small chunks, instead of reacting in panic later.

More importantly, she was shifting from *survival mode* to *preparation mode* — from asking, "How do I get through this month?" to "How do I build the life I actually want?"

But as Sarah began aiming higher with her goals, she ran into a familiar challenge: how to keep saving without feeling like she was always depriving herself.

She didn't want to become the person who never went out, who skipped every birthday dinner, who said "no" to every joy just to say "yes" to her savings account.

That's when she began practicing balance — not as a perfect equation, but as an evolving practice.

She built "fun money" into her budget each month. Sometimes it went toward concerts or takeout. Other times, it became a spontaneous Saturday adventure. Knowing she had that money set aside gave her the freedom to enjoy it without guilt.

Saving wasn't about saying "no" to everything. It was about saying "yes" to the things that *mattered most* — both now and later.

When she was tempted to overspend on something impulsive, she'd ask herself:
Is this taking me closer to my goals or further away?

That single question helped her pause. Not to shame herself, but to realign.

Some months, she leaned more into saving. Other months, life threw her a curveball and she had to pull back. But the balance came from flexibility, not rigidity.

One evening, Sarah looked over her list of future goals and smiled. Some of them still felt far away — like buying a home or retiring comfortably. But they no longer felt impossible.

She had learned that building a sustainable financial future wasn't about being perfect. It was about being *present* — checking in with herself, making space for joy, adjusting when needed, and always remembering the "why" behind the work.

Because the future isn't some far-off finish line. It's made in moments like these — with each decision, each dollar saved, each plan adjusted.

Sarah was no longer afraid of what lay ahead. She was designing it — one thoughtful step at a time.

Section 10.3 – Maintaining Financial Independence

There was a time when Sarah believed financial independence was a finish line—some magical point where everything was paid off, savings accounts were full, and she'd never have to worry about money again.

But now, years into her journey, she understood it differently. Financial independence wasn't about having it *all* figured out. It was about building a life where money no longer dictated her every decision. It was about stability, options, and freedom—not perfection.

It was also something that had to be *maintained.*

After building her emergency fund, paying off her credit cards, and reaching a level of financial comfort she had never experienced before, Sarah found herself in unfamiliar territory. She had space. She had breathing room. But with that new comfort came a subtle sense of uncertainty: *What now?*

The first thing she realized was that true independence meant always having a safety net—not just for today's emergencies, but for tomorrow's uncertainties. She didn't stop contributing to her emergency fund once she reached her goal. Instead, she added to it slowly over time, letting it grow quietly in the background.

Not because she lived in fear, but because she respected the peace that cushion gave her.

She also created "mini nets"—small savings accounts for specific things that could otherwise throw her off course. Car repairs. Pet emergencies. Job transitions. She learned that financial independence wasn't just about avoiding debt; it was about planning ahead for life's curveballs.

And with each account, each deposit, she deepened her own trust in herself.

But Sarah also knew that staying independent required staying *informed.*

She remembered how lost she'd felt when she first started budgeting—Googling basic terms, trying to decipher investment jargon, unsure if she was making the right choices. Back then, learning about money had felt intimidating, almost like learning a second language.

Now, it felt empowering.

She started setting aside time each month to read a personal finance article, watch a video from someone she trusted, or check out a podcast on budgeting or investing. It didn't have to be hours—sometimes it was just 20 minutes while folding laundry. But it kept her mind engaged and her skills sharp.

Financial literacy had become part of her identity. Not because she wanted to be an expert, but because she wanted to keep growing. And in a world where money rules so many things, she wanted to make sure it *never* ruled her again.

She also talked more openly about money—with friends, with family, even with coworkers in trusted conversations. The more she learned, the more she shared. And the more she shared, the more confident she became.

Still, one of the most important lessons Sarah learned about maintaining financial independence had nothing to do with spreadsheets or interest rates.

It had to do with *celebration.*

For a long time, she had been so focused on fixing problems and reaching goals that she forgot to pause and actually feel proud of herself.

So, she started marking milestones.

When she hit her goal of three months of living expenses saved, she took herself out to a nice dinner. When she paid off her last credit card, she bought herself a new pair of shoes—not out of impulse, but out of honor.

Those little moments of celebration weren't just rewards. They were reminders of her resilience.

They told her, "*You did this. You stuck with it. You chose to show up for yourself again and again.*"

She also began journaling once a month, not about what she spent, but about what she was proud of. One month it was sticking to her grocery budget. Another, it was saying no to something that didn't align with her goals.

These reflections became a quiet source of motivation. A reminder that independence wasn't just about numbers—it was about ownership.

Years ago, Sarah had dreamed of a day when she wouldn't feel anxious every time she checked her bank account. Now, she checked it with confidence. Not because she had "arrived," but because she knew how to stay balanced—even when life shifted.

Financial independence wasn't static. It ebbed and flowed, just like everything else.

But she had the habits, the knowledge, and the mindset to adapt.

She had built a life where money worked *for* her, not against her. And in that space, she found something she hadn't expected—joy.

Not just in reaching her goals, but in sustaining them. In knowing she could trust herself to keep moving forward, no matter what came next.

Because real financial independence isn't just freedom from debt or dependence. It's freedom *to choose.* To rest. To grow. To live life on your own terms—and know you've built a foundation strong enough to carry you through.

Conclusion

Your Journey to Financial Peace Starts Now

When you first picked up this book, maybe you felt overwhelmed. Maybe you were behind on bills, living paycheck to paycheck, or facing a mountain of debt that seemed impossible to climb. Or maybe you were simply tired of the constant pressure that comes with trying to make ends meet. Whatever brought you here, I want you to know one thing as we reach the end:

You've already taken the most important step — you've chosen to face your finances head-on.

That alone makes you powerful.

Over the last ten chapters, we've walked through the journey of creating a financial life that works for *you*, not against you. We didn't focus on get-rich-quick schemes or unrealistic promises. Instead, we built something sustainable. Rooted. Human. Practical. Let's take a moment to revisit what you've accomplished and what lies ahead.

A Look Back: The Building Blocks of Financial Transformation

In Chapter 1, we began with the foundational step of understanding your financial reality. That meant assessing where you are, what's coming in, what's going out, and where the financial "leaks" were hiding. This first act of looking honestly at your money—without judgment—laid the groundwork for everything else.

From there, in Chapter 2, we got real about budgeting. Not the kind of restrictive, joyless budget that makes you feel punished. But a bare-bones, minimalist budget that honors your needs first and helps you regain control. We talked about creating a system that fits your life, tracking your spending with intention, and sticking to it through accountability and rewards.

In Chapter 3, we focused on trimming the fat — learning how to cut expenses without sacrificing joy. Whether it was negotiating bills, meal planning, or finding free ways to enjoy your time, you discovered that saving money doesn't have to mean cutting yourself off from happiness.

Then came Chapter 4, where we flipped the script and talked about **increasing** income. Whether through side hustles, negotiating a raise, or selling unused items, you saw how taking initiative and thinking creatively can boost your income in ways that feel achievable and empowering.

Chapter 5 tackled the heavy but critical subject of debt. We broke down the different types, how to build a repayment plan using the snowball or avalanche method, and, most importantly, how to avoid falling back into debt once you've escaped it.

In Chapter 6, we explored how to build an emergency fund — the financial cushion that turns chaos into calm. You saw how small habits, automatic transfers, and a little consistency can lead to peace of mind and true security, even when money is tight.

Next, in Chapter 7, we turned to your credit score — that elusive, often intimidating number that holds real power over your financial opportunities. You learned how to understand, fix, and maintain your credit in a way that builds long-term trust with lenders and opens doors to better options.

In Chapter 8, we widened the lens and looked toward the future. We discussed how to save, invest in small amounts, and plan for retirement — even if you feel broke right now.

The key takeaway? It's not about how much you start with. It's about *starting*.

Then, in Chapter 9, we talked about something rarely addressed in personal finance books: the emotional side of money. We walked through the ways anxiety, shame, and comparison can derail our progress — and how mindset shifts, affirmations, and self-compassion are essential tools in maintaining momentum.

Finally, Chapter 10 brought it all together. You learned how to build a sustainable financial plan — one that adapts with your life, includes space for celebration, and helps you prepare for long-term goals while staying grounded in the present.

Small Steps, Big Impact

If there's one thread that connects everything in this book, it's this: **Small steps create big change.**

Too often, we wait until we have "enough" — enough money, time, energy, knowledge — to make a move. But real change begins when you do *one thing*. When you open your bank account and face the numbers. When you cancel that unused subscription. When you save $5. When you make a phone call to negotiate a bill. When you track what you spend for one week.

These small acts, repeated with consistency and grace, are what transform your financial life.

You don't need to be perfect. You don't need to have all the answers. You don't need to overhaul your entire budget in one night. You just need to begin — and then begin again, even when you fall off.

Progress is rarely linear. Life will interrupt your plans. Unexpected bills will show up. You'll have good months and hard months. That's normal. What matters is that you keep showing up for yourself.

Because you deserve a life that feels financially peaceful. You deserve to rest without guilt. You deserve to stop constantly calculating whether you can afford gas, groceries, or a night out with friends. You deserve to feel *safe* — not because you have everything figured out, but because you've built habits and systems that support you, even when life gets hard.

You're the Author Now

If this book has shown you anything, I hope it's this: You are not powerless. You are not doomed by past mistakes. You are not behind.

You're in motion. You're learning. You're taking action.

Whether you're at the very beginning or somewhere in the middle of your journey, you are building something valuable — not just a budget or a savings account, but *confidence. Resilience. Freedom.*

You're rewriting the story of your money.

And the best part? You're the one holding the pen.

What to Do Next

You might be wondering, "What should I do now?" And the answer is simple: keep going.

Go back to the chapter that hit hardest for you and re-read it. Revisit your budget and adjust it for this month. Set a small savings goal. Open that investment account you've been avoiding. Have that honest conversation with yourself — or your partner — about where you're heading financially.

And as you do it, *celebrate*. Seriously. Every step counts.

Made a grocery list before shopping? That's a win. Tracked your spending for three days in a row? Win. Paused before making a purchase and asked, "Do I really need this?" Win.

Your financial life is built in moments like these — quiet, steady decisions that add up to a very loud kind of freedom.

Final Words of Encouragement

Financial change is not just about money. It's about healing. It's about hope. It's about finally stepping into the version of yourself who feels steady, supported, and in charge of their life.

It doesn't happen all at once. But it *does* happen. And it can happen for you.

So, when doubt creeps in — when the numbers feel too big, or your progress feels too small — come back to this truth:

You are capable.
You are worthy.
And you are not alone.

This book was never about giving you a magic formula. It was about giving you tools, stories, and strategies to help you believe in yourself again. To remind you that you can do hard things — especially the kind that bring you peace.

Your financial freedom isn't on the other side of some big, dramatic moment. It's already in motion — in every choice you make from here on out.

So, take a breath. Take a step. And keep going.

You've got this.
The future is yours to build.

Made in the USA
Monee, IL
04 November 2026

67380063R00108